LOOKING FOR LYRICS

WOW!

**Building Bridges**

**Edited by Vivien Linton**

First published in Great Britain in 2009 by:

Young**Writers**

Young Writers
Remus House
Coltsfoot Drive
Peterborough
PE2 9JX
Telephone: 01733 890066
Website: www.youngwriters.co.uk

# Foreword

Young Writers was established in 1991 to nurture creativity in our children and young adults, to give them an interest in poetry and an outlet to express themselves. Seeing their work in print will encourage them to keep writing as they grow, and become our poets of tomorrow.

Selecting the poems has been challenging and immensely rewarding. The effort and imagination invested by these young writers makes their poems a pleasure to enjoy reading time and time again.

# Contents

# The Poems

# In A Split Second

Isn't it funny
how this play ends in tragedy?
It was a lie from the very beginning,
right up until you delivered the final line.
And you see
me as the girl who barely scratched your heart
But I see
you as the boy who ripped my life apart.

And it's funny how in a split second
you became everything.

Oh when you look at me
you see the girl I was pretending to be.
You see the girl you thought as me;
the girl I became for you and me.

Isn't it funny
how I watched you from afar?
I always imagined my life would be complete
with you on my arm.
Can you tell me
what happened and what went wrong?
How we turned something so right
into something so wrong?

And it's funny how in a split second
you became everything.

Oh when you look at me
you see the girl I was pretending to be.
You see the girl you thought was me;
the girl I became for you and me.

It's funny how in a split second
you became everything to me.
It's funny how in a split second
you became everything I need.
It's funny how you see me now
so differently.

**Holly Drummond (15)**

**1**

# Bring It On!
# (aka Message To The Bullies)

Whatever you have planned for me,
I'm ready;
I'm not bein' a fool no mo',
No longer naïve,
See now I'm ready to take you on,
So bring it on!

It took so long for me
To finally come to see
What you were tryin' to do,
I can't believe I eva trusted you,
See now I know,
So don't try to act as though
You didn't see this ahead,
Go play your games with someone else instead!

I gave you chances,
Forgave you so many times,
Gotta be more careful,
I guess I just missed the signs.

When people try to hold you down
And it feels as though you're gonna drown,
Believe in yourself and speak your mind,
Don't be the one to be left behind,
Say, 'Bring it on, bring it on! Yeah, bring it on!'

And when you've lowered all your shields
And you're tired of cryin' bitter tears,
Don't let them take over your life,
'Cause all they'll do is cause you strife,
Tell them, 'Bring it on, bring it on! Yeah, bring it on!'

I forgave you time after time and then
You went behind my back and did it again,
How many more nights did you expect me to spend
Cryin', dyin', still I kept on tryin',
To see the good in you,
It didn't work, so from now on you and me are through.

When people try to hold you down,
And it feels as though you're gonna drown,
Believe in yourself and speak your mind,
Don't be the one to be left behind.
Say, 'Bring it on, bring it on! Yeah, bring it on!'
And when you've lowered all your shields
And you know you've cried too many tears,
Just let it out - now scream!
Let go, move on, bring it on! Yeah, bring it on!

So many times you lied to me,
So many times I tried to be,
Loyal to you, but you were never
Loyal to me, a good friend to me.
So many times you let them push you,
So many times you claimed you were through,
Too many times you needed to move on,
Let go of your fears and tell them, 'Bring it on!'

When people try to hold you down
And it feels as though you're gonna drown,
Believe in yourself and speak your mind,
Don't be the one to be left behind.
Say, 'Bring it on! Bring it on! Yeah, bring it on!'
And when you've lowered all your shields
And you know you've cried too many tears,
Just let it out - now scream!
Let go, move on, bring it on! Yeah, bring it on!

Too many times, too many times,
Too many times, too many times,
Bring it on, bring it on,
Bring it on, bring it on, *bring it on!*

**Lauren Finlay (15)**

# Theory Of The Man

(Peace y'all
Dunno howta start this
One stage, one man, one mind is one of a kind . . .
An' *boom,* the beat starts, keep heart 'n' don't fart) pause . . .
Let's get 'em, Nick . . . get 'em Nick . . . Nick
Let's get 'em, Nick . . . get 'em Nick . . . Nick
Let's get 'em, Nick . . . get 'em Nick.

I'ma here
music in my mind, why?
Why, cos music is the saviour of the blind.
An' this is my time.
Time to shine, this ain't rappin'
this music they say poetry in motion.
I'm a teenage narrator,
my style's great, I ain't
no ordinary teen that you have seen.
Nicknamed Door, you say, 'Wot for?'
Well that's a tale for tomorrow.
Let's forward to the tale that follows. Tale that follows.

Well, I grew up in the village de la lea Marston
An' I were schooled at Shustoke, it's not far son.
Me mom, dad, two sisters 'n' twin brovver
I was raised, have fun, work hard
Don't get in trouble
Do your homework
'N' I did that 'n' now I find myself at Solihull School,
                                but I feel a fool . . .
cos all I want is a little Cheddar cheese,
no, make that a lot cos I'm lovin' the breeze.
'N' when I'm older I will work hard for the fees.
I'm sittin' here now, achin' from rugby.
Old solts for life, but damn, I can't do anymore press-ups,
I'm sooo messed up.
They called me Mo-r-ris if that ain't clear, they called me Morris.
They say, Nick, great wizard, you got the mad, fat fluid
when you rhyme, you lizard
get into it, cos right now, the world is mine.

Whose world is this?
I'm capable of anything (its mine, it's mine, it's mine).
Whose world is this?
You're capable of everything.
It's yours, it's yours, it's yours, it's yours.
Whose world is this?
We're always capable of everything . . . it's ours, it's ours.

And he said, 'Ye I'ma on my way to diamond rings
In da land of de blind
The man wid one eye is the king . . .'

**Nicholas Morris (15)**

# Seeing

It's not fair,
I don't want you to stare,
Cos far, far away
Someone wants me to stay.
I'm seeing,
I'm seeing a different kind of person.
She's stronger, closer
And better than you!
I've been gone from time to time,
Can't wait for that wedding bell to chime . . .
To ring, ring again,
You're just one big pain in my life now,
I'm seeing,
I'm seeing a different kind of person.
She's stronger, closer
And better than you!
Seeing is believing,
Seeing is believing . . .
And I don't believe in you!
Seeing my new girl is fine,
Knowing that you won't cross the line.
Seelng, seeing . . .
A girl.

**Ashley Webb (12)**

# Take My Hand

Standing underneath your window
I don't care if it rains or snows
I can tell by your tears that you're sad
Crying about what you once had.

Once so pure and full of life
Now just like a hurt, widowed wife
You feel like your heart has gone
Like the light that once shone.

Take my hand, hold it tight
We'll leave this land in the night
Don't look back, not today
Like the shadows, we'll fade away
We're not gonna get hurt no more
Walk away and shut the door
Hand in hand, side by side
We'll walk away with our pride.

And then you looked down without a care
You saw that I was still sitting there
A tear was running down your cheek
In total silence, you couldn't speak.

You know I would be there till the end
'Cause I'll always be your friend
I'll see everything you will see
We will walk away and will be free.

Take my hand, hold it tight
We'll leave this land in the night
Don't look back, not today
Like the shadows, we'll fade away
We're not gonna get hurt no more
Walk away and shut the door
Hand in hand, side by side
We'll walk away with our pride.

It seems like this world moves so fast
Nothing good ever seems to last
But all the bad things seem to stay
It's like they will never go away

We're going to break our chains and disappear
Spread our wings and show no fear
Let's set off and just keep going
We don't need a heading, we don't need any knowing

Take my hand, never let go
'Cause if you do, we'll never know
If we turn the world around and make it good
Like everyone wishes they could
Take my hand and fly away
We'll leave the pain finally.

**Tom Still (18)**

# Cara

Cara, where are your hopes and dreams?
Your happiness ripped at the seams.
I don't understand what you've done to yourself.
Believe me, it's not always a walk in the park,
But don't leave yourself in the dark,
As life goes on, we all
Rise and fall with the tide,
And Cara,
I didn't have to look too far.
I turn the corner, there you are.
Run away again and I'll surely die.
Cara, don't pull yourself apart,
Cara, when the world is your friend, world is your friend,
Cara, we all love you just the way you are.
Cara, don't leave me, don't leave me.
Cara, please put the knife away,
You're not supposed to die today.
Things will get better if you only wait.
Cara, don't pull yourself apart,
Cara, when the world is your stage, world is your stage,
Cara, we all love you just the way you are,
Cara, don't leave me, don't leave me,
Cara.

**Rachel Jacquest (15)**

# Nights Of December

Your hands wrapped around my waist
My arms tangled in chains
The whip in your hand, the smirk on your face.
It's obvious you enjoy my pain.
As I walk in the rain
I can feel you drag me down,
I feel I have to leave this town without you.

Do you remember
The nights of December?
The month where everything changed.
You've turned into a demon,
I've turned into a shattered angel.
We've turned into something that's dead.

You're just a sick sadist
I'm just completely naïve,
Your choking hand proves it,
It's clear to me, you enjoy my pain.
As I walk in the rain
I can feel you drag me down.
I feel I have to leave this town without you.

Do you remember
The nights of December?
The month where everything changed.
You've turned into a demon,
I've turned into a shattered angel.
We've turned into something that's dead.

What happened to times I used to cheer?
It's all been replaced by a terrible fear.
Where are the times I used to be high?
These days all I do is cry,
Cry, cry, cry, lie, lie, lie,
Die, die, die, fly, fly, fly.

Do you remember
The nights of December?
The month where everything changed.
You've turned into a demon,

I've turned into a shattered angel.
We've turned into something that's dead.

Do you remember
The nights of December?
The month where everything changed.
You've turned into a demon,
I've turned into a shattered angel.
We've turned into something that's dead.

**Chloe Gilholy (17)**

# Our World Is Brighter Than You Think

Blue skies into the morning
Dark skies into the night
But when I look up I know
Everything's gonna be alright.

You can save me from the darkness
You can shade me in the sunshine
When I look deep into your eyes I know
We're gonna do just fine

I bet you're wonderin' what on earth I'm thinking
Well I'll tell you the reason why
We all live under the same sky
So our destinies entwine

The rain falls down in the winter
When the skies darken all around
The sun shines down in the summer
But beams without a sound

I bet you're wonderin' why our skies are so cloudy,
Each cloud is a memory,
Each cloud your reverie

Blue skies into the morning,
Dark skies into the night
When I look up into the clear sky
I know our world is pretty bright.

**Jessica Bracey (16)**

# A True Legend

Michael Jackson, who? Yeah, he's the king.
The reason for good music, it revolved around him.
The giving, the loving, he was the true king,
You see what I'm tryna say is, just bow to a legend.
For a second let your thoughts be on this passing legend,
I appreciate him, I appreciate them.
Who's them?
The Jackson family for always giving forever, till no end.

And when my days were cold and so bitter
I'd play MJ's music, tracks like 'Thriller',
And listen to his sad words from 'You Are Not Alone',
And bury them in my mind, for now, my hero is gone,
And I'd dance to 'Billie Jean' and try out the famous moonwalk,
Letting the music sink in, and my tears, they'd never stop,
And though I was born back in '95, I'd skim through music
                                        back from '75,
And watch him dance in the Jackson Five,
Singing 'I'll Be There', I loved watching him live.

He made the world dance, he made us sing,
Joining God's great big family with tracks like
'Heal The World', making us believe
That it don't matter if you're black,
No it don't matter if you're white,
What matters in what's inside,
So I'ma sing this freestyle.

MJ you were the one that showed me
That I can be who I wanna be,
And every day when I got bullied,
And every day when I was worried,
I turned to your music,
Dancing and singing, you see no one could quite sing like you did.
What a loss now that you're gone,
My tears won't stop and I feel alone,
But your legacy will live on,
And you'll live in our hearts,
The king that tried to better us,
As no one can thrill us like MJ dancing the 'Thriller',

Or quite do the moonwalk like he did in 'Billie Jean'.
Or give as much to charity, like the 300million he donated.

We all know you tried to change the world
To make it a better place.
Now I look up in the sky and hope that you're in a better place.
So let's bow to him, for losing him was such a grief,
The king of pop, the loving and giving, the legend that lived.

**Shormee Aziz (14)**

# Now You're Dead

Now you're dead, do you think that
now you're dead, your last celebration
of the life you lived, your final monument
can be desecrated, your name wiped off
by a crowd of rubber trainers
and a crowd of no respect
and then we walk, and don't listen
to those who can speak no longer
to the heroes who live, way down under
while we talk and we strut and we lay your lives down
in front of ours, your trail laid asunder

Question: are you really that much better
than the older generation?
Are our words so much slicker than the elderly bicker?
Are you really that much cooler than a soldier laid in squander?

Do you really think that you're respecting the unloved others?

Now you're dead, do you think that
now you're dead, your last celebration
of the life you lived, your final monument
can be desecrated, your name wiped off
to be unknown forever
so children of the west
teach yourselves
how to truly love
those laid to rest.

**Jack Bradley (14)**

**11**

# Goodbye

Standing in the terminal
Wavin' our goodbyes,
I hate seeing you cry,
Seems such a shame that I have to go,
But long distance is the only way we know.

I promise I'll call,
No I'll never forget you
Even when we're miles apart,
Whether there's snow or there's rain
Or the sun shines bright,
You'll always be in my heart,
Just seems like goodbye's too hard.

It's been half an hour
Since I left,
There are tears in my eyes.
Seems such a shame that I have to go,
But long distance is the only way we know.

I promise I'll call,
No I'll never forget you
Even when we're miles apart,
Whether there's snow or there's rain
Or the sun shines bright,
You'll always be in my heart,
Just seems like goodbye's too hard.

I promise I won't forget you
When the sun shines bright,
When the rain falls hard,
You're the one I want,
And in the winter snow,
You're the one I want to hold.

I promise I'll call,
No I'll never forget you
Even when we're miles apart,
Whether there's snow or there's rain
Or the sun shines bright,
You'll always be in my heart,
Just seems like goodbye's too hard.

**Amy Ray (12)**

# Don't Ever Bother Coming Back

Don't mess me around, but even if you do
You won't get me down, I'm not afraid of you
'Cause I'm stronger now, now that we are through
Without a doubt, doubt, doubt
I was your girl, but I guessed right from the start
That we weren't gonna work, and then we fell apart
I was the one who got hurt, boy, you broke my heart
Without a word, word, word

Now you're gone, guess we were wrong
I never should've put up with all of that
I've moved on, and now I'm strong
Don't ever bother coming back

When you left me, I didn't know what to say
Thought we were meant to be, but then you walked away
But now I see, to you it was just a game
Now I'm free, free, free
And so, I'm leaving you behind
I'm on my own, but baby, I know I'll be fine
I'm better off alone, without you in my life
Now I know, know, know

Now you're gone, guess we were wrong
I never should've put up with all of that
I've moved on, and now I'm strong
Don't ever bother coming back

You treated me bad, and now we're done
I guess I'm kinda glad, that you're not the one
I don't understand why I wanted you once
You weren't a real man, man, man,
 A real man, man, man.

**Alaina Dudhia (14)**

# A Tale Of Luck

I'm in need of a little luck,
Things have happened and run amok.
I need the help of leprechaun gold,
That's the way to go, I'm told.

I know my life's not bad
But again, there's nothing good.
I appreciate the people I have,
And that I know I should.

I know life shouldn't suck,
But what else can I do?
I just need a little luck,
That's why I turned to you.

I know that it's a sin
To wish that I had more,
It seems that you get everything
And I'm left outside your door.

Luck said . . .

The grass is greener, is what luck said,
Greener than yours, but it's in your head.
You get the same amount of luck,
It's the way that you use it which makes life suck.

You always want more
And appreciate none,
So your luck seems divided,
One by one.

But open your eyes
And then you'll see
You get the same luck
As everybody.

Don't feel so down
'Cause someday you'll find
That luck that I gave you,
And how I was so kind.

**Loi Yau (15)**

# Thinking Of You

I'm sitting here, all alone
Why did you leave me
Why did you go?
You know I loved you
And I always would
But then you upped and left me
And now you're gone for good
And baby . . .

Days may come
And days may go
But that won't bring you back
Days may warm and
Nights grow cold
It's the same old song
I just wish I'd stopped to say . . . I love you
Mmm . . . I love you.

I cross the hall to your room
It's just how you left it
Reminds me of you
Man, I wish I'd taken time to
Kiss you goodbye that day
I thought you'd be here when I got back
Didn't think you'd have gone away.

Days may come
And days may go
But that won't bring you back
Days may warm and
Nights grow cold
It's the same old song
I just wish I'd stopped to say . . . I love you
Mmm . . . I love you.

I say a prayer just for you
I hope you're safe and sound somewhere
Where the skies are blue
Cos then maybe I can smile
Even though you're gone for good
Even though you're gone for good.

**Kerry Burns (17)**

# Loving You

You look at me
With that old smile.
Every time I see you
It makes my life worthwhile.
All I want is your true love,
But all I need is you there.

You come across as someone shy
But across the hall you catch my eye.
You wonder why I love you,
You wonder why I care,
But as long as I'm with you,
My love's always there.

I can take anything
When I'm with you.
You make me feel stronger
When you say you love me too.
My love won't fade
Because I love you till the very end of day.

You come across as someone shy
But across the hall you catch my eye.
You wonder why I love you,
You wonder why I care,
But as long as I'm with you,
My love's always there.

Yes I love you till
The very end of day.
La, la, la,
The very end of day,
Cos I'm loving you.

**Emily Pilbeam (12)**

# Stars

Nothing's really perfect
Until you see it for what it is
And it's only what you want to see,
Because if you ever cared,
I wouldn't be standing in the rain,
Waiting on you to call . . .

I had the time of my life
When you were part of it,
You were my brightest star
And like a shooting star I fell,
But I can see you fading now . . .

And no, baby, you weren't perfect,
But you always took my breath away.
Now that you've let me down,
Because I've been waiting
For you to come back round,
Looks like we're not worth fighting for . . .

I had the time of my life
When you were part of it,
You were my brightest star
And like a shooting star I fell,
But I can see you fading now . . .

In the haze I forgot your face,
But every dream I have brings you back
And with every smile and tear
I ever gave you, now I want them back
Because it's the only way I can
Shut you out and say goodbye,
Goodbye, goodbye, goodbye . . .

I had the time of my life
When you were part of it,
You were my brightest star
And like a shooting star I fell,
But I can see you fading now . . .

**Charlotte Macdonald (13)**

# Solid Ground

You've got me, got me good,
I'm not behaving the way I should,
I feel this way whenever you're around,
I don't know what to do,
Whenever I'm alone with you,
Could someone put me back on solid ground?

I can't believe we're here tonight,
I have to overcome this sense of fright.
I know we're both afraid of problems we may have made,
Both hoping it will all turn out alright . . .

You've got me, got me good,
I'm not behaving the way I should,
I feel this way whenever you're around,
I don't know what to do,
Whenever I'm alone with you,
Could someone put me back on solid ground?

I'm gazing deep into your eyes,
That look of love and passion you can't hide.
I hope you cannot see what you have done to me,
I always want you right here by my side.

You've got me, got me good,
I'm not behaving the way I should,
I feel this way whenever you're around,
I don't know what to do,
Whenever I'm alone with you,
Could someone put me back on solid ground?

The only person that I need is you,
I wish we could stay here the whole night through,
I know you love me so, but now you have to go,
I really hope I get to see you soon . . .

You've got me, got me good,
I'm not behaving the way I should,
I feel this way whenever you're around,
I don't know what to do,
Whenever I'm alone with you,
Could someone put me back on solid ground?

**Alison Scott (12)**

# Puppet Strings

She always walks alone,
Though others are so near,
Wearing a plain white dress
Sewn from her isolated fear.
Controlled by malevolent fingers,
Dreams slowly fading away,
In the darkness that still lingers,
Erasing her innocence each day . . .

But one day, she'll fly away
Somewhere bright, no more grey
And one day she'll spread her wings,
Free, from her puppet strings.

Drowning in her sea of sorrow,
Her struggle to escape,
Scared she'll never see tomorrow,
Could it be too late?
Porcelain and hollow,
Falling faster than the angel's tears,
No one to turn to or follow,
She fears one day she'll disappear . . .

But one day, she'll fly away
Somewhere bright, no more grey
And one day she'll spread her wings,
Free, from her puppet strings

Free, from her puppet strings
Free, from her puppet strings . . .

**Crystal Rodrigues (16)**

**21**

# War

Don't pretend you don't want to,
Because I know you want to

One death becomes millions
One betrayal becomes demolition

Just sing this now
why did we have this war
who was it really for?
I swore the past to change
because I never wanted to hurt you

Fun on the beach
became a playing battlefield

what's wrong with the world?
We have all failed.

Just sing this now
why did we have this war
who was it really for?
I swore the past to change
because I never wanted to hurt you

Where is all the love?
Just put down your gloves
why don't you feel the way I do?

War is over
please
not another
not another

Just sing this now
why did we have this war
who was it really for?
I swore the past to change
because I never wanted to hurt you

(Repeat chorus)

Where is all the love?
Just put down your gloves
why don't you feel the way I do?

**Luke Lawton (16)**

# Take Me To Wonderland

When your eyes met my eyes
I was feeling anaesthetised
You captivated my heart
That now controls my mind
I can't stop thinking of you
Every moment in time

Hold my hand
Make me smile
I'm hypnotised
For a glorious while
So sweep me up
And take me there
To a wonderland (wonderland)
Only we know where

So we got in a little boat
And we sailed out to sea
Because nothing else mattered
When it was just you and me
It's a broken milestone
And a door with no key

Hold my hand
Make me smile
I'm hypnotised
For a glorious while
So sweep me up
And take me there
To a wonderland (wonderland)
Only we know where . . .

**Maisie-Jane Baker (14)**

# The Guy

We're sat here like couples do,
Except there's something not quite right
Between me and you,
My friends say just dump the guy,
But how could I leave
This one big lie?

He couldn't be right,
He couldn't win the fight,
I couldn't turn a blind eye
To the guy, to the guy,
To the guy, to the guy.

And when I need to let go
I will, not for now though,
But tell me,
Did you ever love me?
Did you ever, ever love me?
Ooh, tell me.

He couldn't be right,
He couldn't win the fight,
I couldn't turn a blind eye,
To the guy, to the guy,
To the guy, to the guy.

Cos he's slipping through my fingers,
Me and the guy just linger,
And you have nothing left to say,
Just please go away,
I have nothing left to say,
I've never felt this way
About the guy.

He couldn't be right,
He couldn't win the fight,
I couldn't turn a blind eye
To the guy, to the guy,
To the guy, to the guy.

**Tegan-Rose Haines (14)**

# Classified

A couple of friends joined the force
I joined the at training way up north
It was different up there
They made us shave off all our hair
They never treated us with much respect
We couldn't understand their dialect
But they taught us how to fight
And they were deploying us that very night

And I wish that I could tell you
How I broke my little toe
But that rocky training course
Took place so long ago
And I could say it with such pride
But I can't . . . it's classified

I remember over in Vietnam
In a prison where we ate scraps of ham
And the guards around us wore fur
Even the guy with the 30 calibre
Their English was terrible anyway
And it didn't matter what they'd say
We never had a fright
Because we always lived through another night

And I wish that I could tell you
How I broke my little toe
But that rocky training course
Took place so long ago
And I could say it with such pride
But I can't . . . it's classified

And I remember that sunny day
Where we left the place on that old freight train
I wouldn't miss it all that much
Because I'd be stuck forever on a wooden crutch

And I remember some of the men who had died
But now their names are all . . . classified.

**Jonathan Chadwick (14)**

# The One Girl In My Life

There was this girl I used to know, I loved her and still do.
But she never really knew it, and my love grew and grew.

There was this one time we got quite close, but nothing ever happened.
As time dragged on I thought that this was the end.

She was the one girl in my life, the only one I trusted.
I tried to keep it a secret, didn't want to get busted.

It didn't really work, everyone found out.
I thought there was no chance, my life had filled with doubt.

One lad in particular, got annoyed with me.
He wanted her too, but there was no room for three.

I needed to get rid of him, throw him in the bin,
But one problem that I faced, was trying not to sin.

She was the one girl in my life, the only one I trusted.
I tried to keep it a secret, didn't want to get busted.

It didn't really work, everyone found out.
I thought there was no chance, my life had filled with doubt.

I spoke to her in private, got into her mind.
She understood me, she was ever so kind.

She told the other lad to go away, to stop stalking her.
He got a bit upset and started crying, oh what a jerk.

She was the one girl in my life, the only one I trusted.
I then asked her out on a date and bought a ring, diamond encrusted.

We had a lovely time that night, everything was fine,
It was a shame it had to end, she could have come back to mine.

A couple of years later, I proposed to her.
She said yes and made me happier.

We had two kids, a boy and a girl,
The boy was called Jimmy, the girl was called Pearl.

We lived together in a great big house, we were every so happy . . .
Me and her and our two kids.

**James Gray (14)**

# Cinderella

You used to be a hit
Lying on beach sands
Relaxing to the radio
Downing fifty cans
Kicking off your shoes
You're feeling fine
'Til you look at your watch
And realise the time

Cinderella, the shoes are on your feet
But no one's noticed you
Can't even find a seat
Cinderella, the shoes have broken to shards

This isn't fairy-tale land
It's where life gets so hard
Making friends with strangers
Making friends with foes
Keeping on a high
Been through so many lows
I ask you how've you been
You say you're doing fine
'Til you look at your watch
And realise the time

Cinderella, the shoes are on your feet
But no one's noticed you
Can't even find a seat
Cinderella, the shoes have broken to shards

Out all night at parties
Drinking vodka shots
The princess is dead and gone
The story's lost its plot
Your eyes are red and bleary
You used to look so fine
Your watch falls from your wrist
You lose your sense of time.

**Jackson Gregory (15)**

# Come Back

Me and you seemed so right, the days we spent together,
the way you would hold me at night. When you smiled at me
I would start to sing the song you were singing, ooohh, yeah.

But now at night I start to cry and hold onto my pillow tight,
'cause you were like a drug, a drug that I'm still addicted to.
I need you baby, I need you back, 'cause when you left
I died inside and I just can't live without you by my side.
Come back.

You were my light when it got dark, you were my warmth
when it grew cold, ooohhhhh,
you were the reason for me singing, you were the smile I wore.
So please come back, I can't do without you anymore.
Baby, please!

'Cause now at night I start to cry, and hold onto my pillow tight,
'cause you were like a drug, a drug that I'm still addicted to.
I need you baby, I need you back, 'cause when you left
I died inside and I just can't live without you by my side.
Come back.

Please baby, please
I need you. I love you, tell me that you love me too.
I want your arms around me again. I want you
holding me in the night.
I hope that you can still see
That baby, we were meant to be.

'Cause now at night I start to cry, and hold onto my pillow tight,
'cause you were like a drug, a drug that I'm still addicted to.
I need you baby, I need you back, 'cause when you left
I died inside and I just can't live without you by my side.
Come back.

Baby, baby, baby, please, ooohhhh
Ohhh yeah
Baby I love you, baby I need you.
Come back, oh, come back.

**Victoria Lawton (16)**

# The Reality

You saw my face amongst the crowd,
You saw my face,
You saw me bow,
I bathed amongst the waves,
You looked out from the caves
In slow motion.

You like my hair, you like my clothes,
You love my eyes, you love my pose,
You want to be with me.
It's just reality!

You like my hair, you like my clothes,
You love my eyes, you love my pose,
You want to be with me.
It's just reality!

The next day at school
It was just drool
Thinking about you whilst I dreamt,
And in my dream I thought that you and me
Would be together forever, *reality!*

You like my hair, you like my clothes,
You love my eyes, you love my pose,
You want to be with me.
It's just reality!

You like my hair, you like my clothes,
You love my eyes, you love my pose,
You want to be with me.
It's just reality!

I never met you again,
I couldn't take the pain,
I couldn't take the blame,
I didn't play the game,
Ooh, woah, reality.

**Eleanor Bielby (10)**

# I Just Might

She's a heartbreaker,
She knows what to do,
Flash a smile, steal the lights,
Then try and play you.
Gotta use all your strength,
Use all that you got,
To show her you won't be
Something you're not.

I won't change you or break you,
Make you something you ain't.
I won't alter or falter,
Boy you make me feel faint.
You got me tossing and turning,
I can't sleep at night.
I need to say, 'I love you,'
Tonight, baby, I just might.

The way I see it
We're a match made in Heaven,
And on a one to ten,
I'd rate you an eleven.
I feel a deep connection
That we just can't hide.
So tell me how you feel
Way down, deep inside.
You can't deny . . .

I won't change you or break you,
Make you something you ain't.
I won't alter or falter,
Boy you make me feel faint.
You got me tossing and turning,
I can't sleep at night.
I need to say, 'I love you,'
Tonight, baby, I just might.

**Vicky Cloke (14)**

# Right Now

I'll stand close to you, when daytime seems too dark,
When everything has broken up, when sadness leaves its mark.
I'll stand close to you when love has gone away,
When everything has walked on by, you know that I will stay.

I'll stand by your side, when loss is all you know.
When it seems to you, there's nothing left; there's still a place to go.
I offer you a hand to hold, I offer you a hug when things are rough,
You'll always find space in my arms when nothing else seems enough.

'Cause right now, I'm here,
Let me share your laughter and even every fear.
'Cause you'll stay in my heart,
Forever, together, we'll never be apart.
Right now

I'll walk next to you when you need someone to care,
I understand if you just need someone there.
I'll walk next to you, when your heart seems to be breaking,
I'll hold you together, I will stop the aching.

'Cause right now, I'm here,
Let me share your laughter and even every fear.
'Cause you'll stay in my heart,
Forever, together, we'll never be apart.
Right now

'Cause I will think of you every day and every night.
I'll help you with what's wrong, and only leave what's right.

'Cause right now, I'm here,
Let me share your laughter and even every fear.
'Cause you'll stay in my heart,
Forever, together, we'll never be apart.
Right now

Right now. Right now. Right now.
Right now.

**Hannah Pryal (13)**

# My Perfect Lover

I stare out of the window, staring into the space above me,
I look up and see the moonlight clear as you to me.
You look at my picture,
You say, I need ya.

You and me,
Together for eternity,
We were made,
Two hands to hold.
One heart was given
To someone else to find,
Combined.

I will never forget you,
The one who protected you,
I will never regret you,
My perfect lover.

Together is where we belong,
Forever is just a word in a song.
It takes three seconds to say I love you,
It takes a lifetime to prove ya do-o-o.

Did I do something wrong?
You put these stupid words in a song.
I hate you, I love you, I adore you,
Which one should I believe?

Together is where we belong,
Forever is just a word in a song.
It takes three seconds to say I love you,
It takes a lifetime to prove ya do-o-o.

I will never forget you,
The one who protected you,
I will never regret you,
My perfect lover.

**Jaimie Lane (13)**

# Addicted To You

I told all my friends we'd broke up
And we could finally get on with life
And could go on girly nights out
Life without all that strife

But soon we are texting again
And I realise I need you
We always pass each other
And I realise I always knew

I'm addicted, addicted
Yeah, addicted to you
But sometimes I wish I could get my point through
But I knew you'd catch on
When our relationship grew

Hanging out feels much better
When I know you're there
I'm wearing your old sweater
While chatting to my mate, Clare

I'm addicted, addicted
Yeah, addicted to you
But sometimes I wish I could get my point through
But I knew you'd catch on
When our relationship grew

But I feel sometimes you're over-protective
I'm not allowed to go anywhere without you knowing
I need some freedom with my old mates
I'm not that outgoing anymore, like before

Now not so addicted to you
You don't even have a clue
Exactly what I went through
Right now I need you to go away
And get outta my head.

**Hannah Cartmill (13)**

# One In A Million

There you were
Standing right in front of me.
You're the one that makes my heart skip a beat
The one who picks me off my two left feet.

Can't you see?
When I look at you in a certain way.
You mean so much more
Than my trembling lips could ever say.

You never understood
I was happy when you were mine.
Now there are only memories left
A heartbroken scar that will heal in time.

The stars shine above in the sky.
You're one in a million.

This crazy feeling seems to make me fly,
You're one in a million,
One in a million.

Yet I can't let go.

This love is so appealing,
Thoughts in my head so mixed up
Yet I listen only to my feelings.

What do I do?
I can't seem to leave this situation.
Without you in my life
Would only cause frustration.

There you are,
Time still seems to move on.
Like the bright, glistening stars
To me, you're one in a million,
One in a million.

**Kay McAdam (18)**

# Messed-Up World

All soldiers go to war
Big explosions, fighting for
Freedom and other things like government

What kind of messed-up world is this?
Is this, is this?
Oh it's a messed-up world
Won't it stop?

All children go to school
It's not that rare at all
But in poor countries it's impossible

What kind of messed-up world is this?
Is this, is this?
Oh it's a messed-up world
Won't it stop?

All footballers kick a ball
Always trying to score a goal
But do they really need to get paid so much?

What kind of messed-up world is this?
Is this, is this?
Oh it's a messed-up world
Won't it stop?

The Queen and government
Work together in parliament
Making big decisions that *should* help us all

What kind of messed-up world is this?
Is this, is this?
Oh it's a messed-up world
Won't it stop?

If we work together we can all
Save this world!

**Harry Palmer (13)**

# Forgotten Memories

Forgotten, forgotten
Forgotten, forgotten

All the memories that we had
Not all of them made us sad
And all the people that we meet
We just meet them on the street

Having hours and hours of fun
Playing with your water gun
Spinning round and round at the park
Scaring each other in the dark

All these forgotten memories
Only make us wake up and see
We are lucky
We are lucky to even have these.

And all the times that we shared
They'll always stay in my head
You just make me smile today
And I will thank you, you looked my way.

I learn from my mistakes
That some memories are fake
You just don't know what to do
And that's when I met you.

All these forgotten memories
Only make us wake up and see
We are lucky
We are lucky to even have these.

All the times we spent together
They build up in my head
It's not to do with the weather
The fact you'll always be dead.

**Jack Norman (14)**

# Exhaustion

You wanna laugh out loud, you wanna scream and shout
But then when you wake up your head is filled with doubt
You didn't go to sleep and you didn't proceed with caution
Because of that you've got this feeling.

You want to crash out big, you wanna sleep and snore
But your three best friends are not wanting you to snore
You didn't go to sleep and you didn't proceed with caution
Because of that you've got the feeling of . . .

Exhaustion
You've got the feeling of exhaustion
You ever had the feeling of exhaustion?
Your current feeling is exhaustion

You tend to stay up late when you are feeling great
But then, when you wake up, then that's the thing you hate
You didn't go to sleep and you didn't proceed with caution
Because of that you've got this feeling.

You always have a drink, you always have a laugh
But when you're dragged out of your bed, you feel the wrath
You didn't go to sleep and you didn't proceed with caution
Because of that you've got the feeling of . . .

Exhaustion
You've got the feeling of exhaustion
You ever had the feeling of exhaustion?
Your current feeling is exhaustion

But then you make a change and really go to bed
And now when you wake up there is no banging head
You said you went to sleep and yes you did proceed with caution
Because of that there is no feeling of . . .

Exhaustion
There is no feeling of exhaustion.

**Dean Garrod (12)**

# Just Let Me Be Me

I want to rap to be with the next stars
So I can buy the latest shoes and cars.
Don't try and change me, let my life be how it's supposed to be
I will do anything to see that pretty smile
I long to see it and I'll make it worthwhile

Even when I'm with my friends walking down the street
You will be the one who I really want to meet
So can you give me your number
So I can stop daydreaming of ya?
Maybe we can go out sometime
Just so I can see those pretty eyes shine
Your voice sounds like how an angel sings
To me you're worth more than anything

I want to rap to be with the stars
So I can buy the latest shoes and cars.
Don't try and change me
Let my life be how it's supposed to be
I will do anything to see that pretty smile
I long to see it and I'll make it worthwhile

I'm like the great white shark and you're the pretty fish
And one day you can be my beautiful little miss
It's like we are the king and queen of the oceans
Now let me see you dance in your funky motions
Together we will be infinity
No one else but you and me

I want to rap to be with the next stars
So I can buy the latest shoes and cars
Don't try and change me, let my life be how it's supposed to be
I will do anything to see that pretty smile
I long to see it and I'll make it worthwhile,
So let me be me.

**Ryan Lalli (12)**

# I Didn't Pay Cupid

Which ass decided to invent this emotion?
Without it everything would run so smooth
No broken hearts
No falling apart

The memories still linger
They make my head spin
I almost regret ever meeting you
Cos I thought what you said was all true
How could I be so stupid?

Which ass decided to invent this emotion?
Without it everything would run so smooth
No broken heats
No falling apart

As if we would last
For some reason
I don't want you in the past
Oh how times change so fast
Almost as if our hearts are black

Which ass decided to invent this emotion?
Without it everything would run so smooth
No broken hearts (no broken hearts)
No falling apart (no falling apart)

People say I'm stupid
But hey, I didn't pay Cupid
I just can't help feeling
That there's a part of me missing
And knowing that I'll never get it back
Is the hardest thing to get over

*No broken hearts*
*No falling apart!*

**Chloe Hill (13)**

# I Wish

I wish I could stay forever and ever, but you see the thing is
It's a little late for expectations. There's nothing you can do
Because I don't wanna be with you any longer.
You broke me, you broke my heart then I grew strong.

There is no other way, I don't wanna do this any more
I have spoken, I mean it, this time it's over, I mean it
It's over this time
I wish it could be different, I wish.

You never knew how to treat me or anyone
You were too overpowering, you hated seeing me with anyone
You wanted to be the only one in my life,
I loved you but now it's time you realised.

There is no other way, I don't wanna do this any more
I have spoken, I mean it, this time
It's over, I mean it, it's over this time
I wish it could be different, I wish.

Would you fall apart the same as I did, would you feel hurt?
You've got all the things I thought I wanted
Say you're sorry as I pace back and forth, I then realised
You weren't perfect, not the guy I thought you were.

There is no other way, I don't wanna do this any more
I have spoken, I mean it, this time
It's over, I mean it, it's over this time
I wish it could be different, I wish.

I've made up my mind, I don't care if you think I'm wrong
You hurt me, you hit me, I'd finally seen your true self
You knocked me down, you made me feel worthless
I tried to leave you, I never got past the door, you hurt me
No one in this world knows you like I do, it's time you stopped
I thought I loved you but I hate you, I just wish you could stop.

**Alice Williams (13)**

# Shadow Soul

In your eyes, I see what you are
It's no surprise, I know you hide
I see inside, I know your truth
You're the one I need, I want you

Shadow soul I know you're there
It's in your eyes, but I don't care
You took my heart and you will see
I must have you, 'cause you've got me
Shadow soul you must be mine, yeah

You pulled my strings, you control me
I played into your dark, dark hands
It's just because you don't understand
I must have you, but you don't see

Shadow soul I know you're there
It's in your eyes, but I don't care
You took my heart and you will see
I must have you, 'cause you've got me
Shadow soul you must be mine, yeah

La, la, la, la, la, la, la, la, la
La, la, la, la, la, la, la, la, la
La, la, la, must have you now
La, la, I know you want me now
La, la, la, we're meant to be now

Shadow soul I know you're there
It's in your eyes, but I don't care
You took my heart and you will see
I must have you, 'cause you've got me
Shadow soul you must be mine, yeah

La, la, la, la, la, la, la, la, la
La, la, la, you shall be mine, yeah.

**Caitlin Mitchell (12)**

# Terri James Memorial

See, I'm breaking apart
so I try to write 'bout your life in a verse.
It hurts to know that you're gone,
I try to forget but you're making it hard.
See, you had a life so painful
but I think that's it over now
so I just think that I might zone it out
because I know that God's just gained an angel.
There's a lot of things that I never say,
like how the days that we spent were the best
but still I'm glad that you're out of the pain
and that you've moved to a better place.
So when my fears hit me bad,
I know that you're watching down on my life
so I just pick up a pen and think
and drop a few tears on a pad.

So I keep my feelings ahead
you were that girl that was always smiling
nothing got you down and so for now
I just can't be dealing with stress.
Sometimes I feel like screaming
because when it gets to my head
I feel like I just wanna give up on life
cos nobody really knows what I'm feeling
so I break down and start crying
just wanna be left on my own
with no one around, not hearing a sound
cos sometimes it really feels like I'm dying
sick and tired of the pain aching.
So I wish that things were OK
or better yet, I wish that you were still here
and me and you could just trade places.

**Thomas Martin (16)**

# Nowhere Left To Run

We're trapped in a corner
The shadows lurking in
We stand side by side
Hoping and praying that the demons would go away

There's nowhere left to run
So take hold of my hand
And never let me go
It's the end of the lie
We will die together (die together)

The blood dripping down my face
As I tried to save my friend
You and I together
Braving this terrible event

There's nowhere left to run
So take hold of my hand
And never let me go
It's the end of the lie
We will die together (die together)

We are dying (we are dying)
Very slowly
We have to suffer the pain
How hard it is to stay alive
Me and you will try

There's nowhere left to run
So take hold of my hand
And never let me go
It's the end of the lie
We will die together (die together)
There's nowhere left to run
So take hold of my hand.

**Caitlin Docherty (12)**

# Real World Justice

I was an innocent girl, crying
The pain was excruciating.
You are the living murderer
Who took away my pumping heart.

You never locked him up for what he did.
I can't believe you, how could you do this?
'Cause this is real world justice,
I didn't know that it would end like this.
I thought that I could find a fix
But I guess that this is just real world justice.

I never found out who you were,
You were in such a furious state.
I didn't get to stay awake,
How could anyone forgive you?

You never locked him up for what he did.
I can't believe you, how could you do this?
'Cause this is real world justice,
I didn't know that it would end like this.
I thought that I could find a fix,
But I guess this is just real world justice.

You, you stabbed me in the heart,
Leaving me bleeding to death.
You laughed and killed me once more
Knowing that you got away with this deadly murder.

You never locked him up for what he did.
I can't believe you, how could you do this?
'Cause this is real world justice,
I didn't know that it would end like this.
I thought that I could find a fix
But I guess this is just real world justice.

**Siân Ellis-Daish (14)**

# 13 Years

This day it stings more than the others,
this pain throbs deeper than before,
this hour's been harder than the previous
cos its power burns me to the core.
This time slowly passing by
does nothing more than make me wanna cry,
this day is harder than before
when battling with the anniversary of your past.
13 years, with you gone now,
13 years without you here,
13 years of getting stronger
and in 13 seconds my strength disappears
just knowing it's been 13 years.
Your smile brought refuge like no other,
your eyes exhausted any fears
and when I think of how you're gone now
I can't help but spill my tears.
Cos this time slowly passing by
does nothing, nothing more than make me wonder why
this day is tougher than the rest
when you're battling with an anniversary
cos you were the best.
13 years, with you gone now,
13 years without you here,
13 years of getting stronger
and in 13 seconds my strength disappears
just knowing it's been 13 years.
And I may not know you now
but I smile knowing that I did somehow
and I may just not know where you are
but I love you, yes I love you
from the bottom of my heavy heart.

**Eleanor Curran (13)**

# This Girl

I met this girl when she came on my street
All I wanted to do was compete
My heart pounced with her sight
So I asked if I could stay the night
I just wanted to give her care
I just wanted to touch her hair
She was fit and she was fine
She was so very divine
I took her to dinner that very next day
I knew my feelings but I could not say
There she was, there was I
If I couldn't tell her then I would die
I met this girl when she came on my street
All I wanted to do was compete
My heart pounced with her sight
So I asked if I could stay the night
When we got back I could see
It don't go together you and me
I said 'bye that very next day
She was so sad she could not say
I went to her house the very next day
Because of what I felt, I should say
You make me feel really good
You make me feel the way I should
I met this girl when she came on my street
All I wanted to do was compete
My heart pounced with her sight
So I asked if I could stay the night
When we got back I could see
It does go together, you and me
I'm in love, don't you see?
I love you, do you love me?

**Ryan Perry (12)**

# If You Only Try

A long time ago I knew a girl
A girl afraid to dream
She never opened her heart
To anyone to make them see
That she could be that someone
Locked in a memory
She didn't know you can make it
If you only believe
You can make your life much better
You can live all your dreams
You can learn how to fly
Once you've spread your wings into the sky
You know that it's not easy
You know it will take time
You know that it will happen
If you only try
A long time ago I knew a girl
A girl who hid away
A girl who just let her emotions
Get in the way
She lived her life in sorrow
For all she had lost
She didn't see that good things happen
Without a cost
She can make her life much better
She can live all her dreams
She can learn how to fly
Once she's spread her wings into the sky
She knows that it's not easy
She knows it will take time
She knows that it will happen
If she only tries.

**Michaela Gibson (17)**

**47**

# A Boy And A Girl

A boy and a girl, the best of friends
From elementary to high school, from beginning to end.
Through all those years their friendship grew,
They both felt the same, but neither knew.
Each waking moment, since the day they met,
They both loved each other, sunrise to sunset.
He was all she had in her terrible life,
He was the one who kept her from her knife.
She was his angel, she made him smile,
Though life threw him pain, she made it all worthwhile.
Then one summer's day things went terribly wrong,
The next few weeks were like a very sad song.
He made her jealous, on purpose he tried,
When the girl asked, 'Do you love her?' on purpose he lied.
He played with jealousy, it was like a game,
Little did he know things would never be the same.
His plan was working, but he had no clue
How wrong things would go, the damage he would do.
One night she broke down, feeling very alone,
Just her and the blade, no one else home.
She dialled his number, she heard his happy tone,
She told him she loved him and hung up the phone.
He raced to her house, just a minute too late,
Found her lying in blood, her heart had no rate.
Beside her a note, in it her confession,
Her love for this boy, her only obsession.
As he read the note, he knelt down and cried,
Grabbed her knife, that night they both died.
She was found in his arms, both of them dead,
Under her note, his handwriting said,
'I loved her so, she never knew
All this time, I loved her too'.

**Emily Magnus**

# There For Me

I thought you were always going to be there for me
But I'm the only thing that's stopping you,
Oh, oh
I never thought you'd miss me
But now I know it was fake,
You were only faithful
To no one but yourself.
I used to think
You didn't like me for who I was,
But I was wrong.
You,
Me,
No one else.
I need my life,
But you and
Me together
Are the perfect couple until eternity.
But I was wrong.
You used to tell me I was your angel,
I was sent from up above,
But when my halo disappeared
There was nothing left,
I was empty.
Friends are there until the end,
But the sun will shine and fade,
And when it fades
You have to let go.
But when the sun shines bright
We will always be
Together forever,
But now I know,
You were always there for me.

**Ellesha King (13)**

# Addicted Again

You're a bad habit
That I can't seem to stop.
I know you're no good for me,
But you're all I've got.
I pull myself away from you
And say I'll never go back,
But it's a perfect white lie,
To hide what I have.

It's addictive, crazy, stupid and fake,
I'm always out here, lonely, no one to face.
I'm always helpless, deserted and all on my own.
But you make me feel loved.

Though there's nothing there at all.
I'm your experiment that went completely wrong.
You're a heartbreaker, love faker,
And there's no turning back.
Looks like I'm stuck
And addicted to you again.

These moments replay
Around in my head,
Those words that you said
Make my heart stop.
I'll always wonder if
It's worth another try,
But for some reason, I just
Can't seem to say goodbye.

And it's addictive, crazy, stupid and fake,
I'm always out here, lonely, no one to face.
I'm always helpless, deserted and all on my own.
But you make me feel so loved.

**Natasha Todd (14)**

# The Doctor And The Space Rap

The Doctor, he's the Time Traveller,
He travels in time and space with Martha.
Monsters, they try to beat him,
But they will never defeat him.

The Doctor is an alien,
He travels all the time,
He is everyone's hero,
And he's definitely mine.

The TARDIS, the Doctor's machine,
The master turned it to a paradox, isn't that mean
Earth known as Planet Three,
The Doctor helps us humans through our history.

The Doctor is an alien,
He travels all the time,
He is everyone's hero,
And he's definitely mine.

It is fun to travel through big space,
But Earth, the Doctor thinks is the bestest place.
Back in time to queens or Henry VIII,
If I could go back to Shakespeare, that would be great.

The Doctor is an alien,
He travels all the time,
He is everyone's hero,
And he's definitely mine.

The Doctor shuts the TARDIS and says goodbye,
The world is all safe as he floats in the sky.
Now all the time travel finishes in a zap,
Thank you for reading . . .
The Doctor and space rap.

**Danielle Owen (13)**

# Staring Me In The Face

It was blank.
A huge empty space,
And it was staring me in the face.

It was blank.
A huge empty space,
And it was staring me in the face.

So then I dunked my hands into the bright green gloop,
Like sticking your head into a bowl of soup.
I splashed the green onto the screen,
It looked much better, if you know what I mean!

It wasn't blank,
Not a huge empty space,
Just a big green blob
Staring me in the face.

I had spoiled it,
My huge empty space.
It was ruined.
So I found some white,
Everything was gonna be alright!

So then I dunked my hands into the new white gloop,
Like sticking your face into a bowl of soup.
Then I splashed the white all over the green,
It looked much better, if you know what I mean!

It was blank.
A huge empty space,
*My* huge empty space,
And it was staring me in the face.
*My* huge empty space,
Just staring me in the face.

**Hannah Linaker (13)**

# Untitled

I suppose you could say love is many things
And everyone can feel it
It isn't made true by flowers and rings
It's how it feels when your heart is hit.

Some people wait for all their lives
Some people search for husbands and wives
But what they don't seem to realise
Is how it can hurt you like the stab of a thousand knives.

We're just going through the motions
Repeating what we've done
Lust and love are just potions
The battle is never won
We need to stop chasing shadows.

I remember it all went sober
A memory from yesterday
It was like we had a phobia
A price we felt we had to pay.

You left me breathless
You left me weak
My legs used to turn to jelly
My mouth unable to speak.

I thought it was forever
I washed the footprints from the sand
It wasn't how love was supposed to be
Here I stand.

I can still remember your beautiful face
The way you used to hold me like there was no tomorrow
I can still feel you in my heart to this day
I'm basking in the everlasting feeling of sorrow . . .

**Amelia Marron (14)**

# As Long As We're Laughing

We could sit outside and watch the sunset
Or we could go down the pub and watch the match
We could stay inside 'til all's forgotten
Or we could sit and talk about the past

If the world was burning I would save you
If the stars burst into flames
If everyone I knew forgot me
I know that you would stay the same

Who knows what might happen?
As long as we're still laughing
You and me, that's all that matters
You and me, that's all that counts

If the world bites and I fall apart
And I feel the planet's out to get me
I know as long as I'm with you
I'm still standing and my head's still up

In a world this big I'm glad I've found you
I don't care what people say
They've got their girls and got their guys but
I don't know if they've felt this way

Who knows what might happen?
As long as we're still laughing
You and me, that's all that matters
You and me, that's all that counts

Another day and you're still here
Another day with a smile on my face
Another day with no fear
Not another day I'd live without you
Cos baby, it's you and me.

**Hayley Clayton (14)**

# You Gotta Be Happy

Ahh, yeah,
You gotta be happy living your life
You gotta scream and shout
And let all that anger out
'Cause everyone knows you've only got one chance
to try to fulfil your dreams
and everyone loves to be happy
so you know what you gotta do!

You gotta be happy every day
You gotta scream and shout
And have fun 'cause everyone knows
To be happy . . . oh.

I'm only 12 and I'm having fun
I've got all the friends I need
My friends are there when I need them, indeed
Sooo!

Oh, oh

It's late at night and it's on a Friday
Everyone's partying tonight
It's fun to muck about
The moon is up and the feeling's just right
And there's no way anyone is going to stop us!
Yeah!

Oh, oh
Oh, oh

You gotta, you gotta
Hey, hey, hey, hey, hey
You gotta, you gotta
Be happy every day!

**Kirsten Rock (12)**

# Keeping Secrets

Nobody tells me anything,
Everyone's keeping secrets.
Nobody tells me anything,
Everyone's keeping things to themselves.

My mum always told me
Never let secrets out,
But there's one problem with me,
I like to scream and shout.

Nobody tells me anything,
Everyone's keeping secrets.
Nobody tells me anything,
Everyone's keeping things to themselves.

I'm no good at secrets,
I always crack and tell,
Most people don't trust me
So all I hear is yell, yell, yell!

Nobody tells me anything,
Everyone's keeping secrets.
Nobody tells me anything,
Everyone's keeping things to themselves.

I am good at one thing though,
I'm really into art,
I always like to lend a hand
For those who aren't so smart.

Nobody tells me anything,
Everyone's keeping secrets.
Nobody tells me anything,
Everyone's keeping things to themselves,
Everyone's keeping things to themselves.

**Samantha Cullen (12)**

# Life Advice 101

Come on all you girls and all you boys,
This is Life Advice 101, make some noise!
We live in today and never look back,
We live for tomorrow,
Not the past,
Remember the moments that were the best,
Forget all the ones that look like the rest.
Can't predict the future,
None of it's true,
Could have a crystal ball,
But you won't get through.
So don't do the drugs,
You'll end up a mess,
Same goes for cheap beer and cigarettes.
Get a good job
With a good pay,
Suck up to your boss
If you want a raise.
We're all gonna die
So let's have some fun!
But please don't forget-
Life Advice 101.

And when your time run's out
There's no need to scream or shout,
We will all end up there,
So let's take time to prepare . . .
One day we will all wake up in the sky,
Run, jump, take a dive and learn to fly.
We'll laugh with the birds and sing happily,
Because now we're all angels . . .
Finally free.

**Leah Greenhalgh (14)**

# What Happened To The Guy I Knew?

I feel a chilly breeze
As we walk among the trees,
I reach for your hand and you pull away,
I try again and you look the other way.
What happened to you?
We used to talk, we used to laugh,
Now you won't even hold my hand.

Your eyes glance past me,
When I look for you, you always shut me out.
I want to help, but how . . . how . . . how?
You close up, you won't talk,
And you stand there, white as chalk.
When I speak to you, you look straight through me.
What can I do? What happened to the guy I knew?

We sit in the living room
Watching TV, there's nothing else to do.
I change the channel from sports to news,
And that doesn't even bother you.
What happened to you?
Now if I dress up for you in my best clothes,
You shake your head and stare at your toes.

And finally now I see,
I know the truth and it still kills me.
How could you do that to me
With everything we have been through?
What happened to you?
You cheated, lied and stole my heart,
I must admit it was a work of art.
I find out in a letter,
And I thought I knew you better.

**Vanessa Brown (16)**

# You Loved Me

I know you're impatient and can't handle lies
But how else do I make you realise
The pain in my chest, in my heart, in my mind?
Rip apart the layers and soon you'll find
That nothing sinks in, nothing's believed
And maybe it'll help you to be more relieved
If I tell you this now, and if you believe it
That nothing I do will ever be free from it
Free from the pain, free from the sorrow
It's hard to take in, it's hard to swallow
But somehow I'll manage and somehow I'll cope
After all - what's the worth of a life without hope?

I thought you told me you loved me?
You make it so hard to believe!
I thought you told me you loved me . . .
The words so hard to conceive.

I know you feel guilty and can't deal with regret
But in this case the best thing to do is forget
That you ever felt this way at all, unless
Your future plan includes sorting out this mess
We call our daily lives, the lives we will lead,
For lack of anything else to do, so we plead
Please do something to make life less dull
While still we live on, activities we'll cull
For lack of promise - no excitement is held
So on and on, our lives we continue to fell
Until nothing is left, just an empty case
And a lone tear, sliding down my face.

I thought you told me you loved me?
I thought you told me you loved me . . .

**Annie Harries (14)**

**59**

# Don't Care

You think . . . that I'm weird
But you don't know much about me
Your friends . . . like to laugh
When they pass me in the street
I don't wear . . . trendy clothes
And I don't wear lots of make-up
But one thing that I know,
I'm gonna be myself.

I don't care what you say
I don't care what you do
Cos I wanna be me
I don't wanna be you.
It's my life, can't you see
That you can't pressure me?
I don't care what you say
When you stare
I don't care.

Look at yourself
What do you see?
When I see myself
I see me.

I don't care what you say
I don't care what you do
Cos I wanna be me
I don't wanna be you.
It's my life, can't you see
That you can't pressure me?
I don't care what you say
When you stare
I don't care.

**Lily Goodwin (14)**

# Make-Believe

They say
Curiosity killed the cat
And to be completely honest, baby,
You're turning me into that,
I didn't want to be nosy,
I didn't want to intrude,
But sweetie, honey, baby,
Do I really mean that much to you?

Is this all just make-believe?
Do you really set out to deceive?
I'm laying shaking and my heart is aching,
You're setting me up to lose.

Misrepresentation and all this concentration,
Damn, doesn't it make you question this one?
I turned a blind eye towards all the signs,
So I've only got myself to blame.

Is this all just make-believe?
Do you really set out to deceive?
I'm laying shaking and my heart is aching,
You're setting me up to -
Tune out, tune out and topic change.
I know exactly what's going on
In that brain of yours,
(Whispers) Just say it, go on,
(Whispers) I dare you to admit it.

Is this all just make-believe?
Do you really set out to deceive?
I'm laying shaking and my heart is aching,

You're setting me up to lose you honey.

**Zoe Small (15)**

# Crash And Burn

The rain is falling down
and clouds move closer now,
your drowning pain is washing me away.
Just one ray of light
can heal our wounds,
I no longer want to fight.

You can say that I'm a fool
but the truth is it's all because of you,
I've been waiting for your love, it's now my turn.
We've always been flying so high
only to fall, crash and burn.

It feels like a losing war,
I'm caught up lying on the floor,
please promise my heart won't suffer anymore.
Just one clear day
can save us from it all
now our edges have started to fray.

Feel like you've locked me out,
you started putting up your defences
long before you could ever give me a chance.
I'll give you everything and more,
just don't show me your fighting stance.

Give me a chance
not your fighting stance.
I need you more now
Than ever before,
Than ever before.

Crash and burn
crash and burn . . .

**Emma Bantleman (18)**

# Medals Of Supreme Awesomeness

I can't bear getting that silver put upon me,
I can't even bear becomin' number three.
I just got to get
On that middle step of the podium.
I deserve to be on the podium.
I always erupt the stadium.
Medals of supreme awesomeness hang upon my wall,
Remembering the days when I was ten feet tall.
I am such an idiot, I should have got rid of them long ago,
But now I'm beggin' you, please don't let my medals go.
I forgot what it feels like to lose;
I even forgot the last time I wasn't in the news.
I just got to be
More than number three in the competition.
I deserve to win the competition,
That is my ultimate mission.
Medals of supreme awesomeness hang upon my wall,
Remembering the days when I was ten feet tall.
I am such an idiot, I should have got rid of them long ago,
But now I'm beggin' you, please don't let my medals go.
My medals of supreme awesomeness,
What it's done to my life I must confess.
I've gone mad,
I'm so sad,
No way to
Fight through.
So 'bye,
Don't lie,
You're happy,
No sappy scene.
I'm gone and so are my medals now!

**Hayleigh Mcaleese (14)**

# Always And Forever

For always and forever
I swear that I'll be true
My heart will beat only for you
For always and forever
My eyes will only see you
To watch you smile and laugh
For the whole day through
For always and forever
We will hold each other close
Time will stand still
When we become us
For always and forever
Together we will be
Nothing will come between us
Because of the strength of we
For always and forever
No harm will come to you
I shall keep you safe
For the whole day through
For always and forever
Happy is what we'll be
You shall never shed a tear
Because of the fun you'll have with me
For always and forever
As constant as the stars
I'll close my eyes
And I'll be wherever you are
For always and forever
Forever will be mine
Forever will be yours
Forever will be ours.

**Hollie Million (15)**

# Untitled

Standing
On
The
Beach
Darkness
Hangs
Above
Me
How
I
Try
To
Reach
The
Shooting
Star
In
The
Sky
I'm
So
Lonely
I
Constantly
Cry
I
Miss
You
More
Every
Day.

**Paige Norman (9)**

# New Kid

I heard that you're the new babe in town,
And you're well tryin' to take my crown.
You think you're a big hit just 'cause you're new,
That don't mean I'm gonna forget my old crew.
Is it 'cause you're not getting any that you act all sleazy?
Maybe if I push my bra up you'll think I'm a girl that plays it easy.
I see you with all those kinda girls around town,
But when you see me, all I get is some frown.
I'm like, 'What are you playin' at man?'
You just seem to get everything you can.
Okay I'll admit, you are quite fit,
But I ain't gonna like you just 'cause of it.
My mates tell me they think you're mad 'cause you like to get drunk
Though my mum says you're nothing but a no good punk.
I decide to talk about it to my sister, Ella,
I tell her that I can't stop thinking about this fella.
She tells me to act as if I don't even know he's alive,
I say, 'I'll give it a go, but how will I survive?'
The next day I see him, and well, I walk straight past,
I see through the corner of my eye, he looks back, at last.
Maybe she was right, maybe this will work,
I couldn't help but get this strong feeling of a quirk.
I then get this text asking if I want to meet at the river,
*Could this be real?* I think, I immediately start to shiver.
It's from that guy, the one I was disregarding.
Now that I see him, I know our friendship is hardening.
We constantly keep meeting and meeting,
I then tell my mates about this guy I've been seeing.
I describe every detail, and then say his name's Lee.
They look at each other oddly and say,
'Girl, that's the one that's been seeing me.'

**Mie Palmer (15)**

# Goodbye

I see you lyin' there
With another girl by you
And you notice me and say, 'I'm so sorry.'
But I don't believe a word you say,
Why don't you get your stuff and get out the door?
I don't want you here in this place,
I don't wanna see your face,
So just get outta this place.

We were perfect together,
So why did you have to be with her?
Yeah, yeah, you used to be the one for me, yeah,
So I guess this is goodbye.

I want you back with me
So we can start all over,
So we can start anew. I love you . . .
I didn't mean a word I said,
But I was just surprised at you.
Why did you do this to me?

We were perfect together,
So why did you have to be with her?
Yeah, yeah, you used to be the one for me, yeah.

Now I have to say that we
Are perfect together,
'Cause we worked it all out.
You are the one for me,
I hope it will never end,
And I just wanted to say that
I love you, I love you,
I love you, I love you!

**Hannah Warrender (9)**

# Catching Love

When love walks through the door,
You pull it close,
You never let go
'Cause you're afraid
It won't come back to you, no, no.

Love is strong, love is cruel,
Don't go wasting it, you fool.
Love comes in and love goes out,
Just don't go fooling about.

When you snatch it close to you
Then you may let loose,
Don't go mental, just keep cool,
Or you'll lead it to a fall.

Love is strong, love is cruel,
Don't go wasting it, you fool.
Love comes in, love goes out,
Just don't go fooling about.

Now you've got it, keep it close,
It's all yours, spoil it, love it,
Do everything with it please,
Don't let it go again.

Love is strong and love is cruel
Don't go wasting it, you fool.
Love comes in and love goes out,
Just don't go fooling about.

Love is hard, love is nice,
Now you've got it, have a good life.
Yeah, yeah.

**Alice Gallienne (12)**

# I've Been Down The Road Before

It's a good life
When you close your eyes
And dare to dream.

No expectations
Or complications,
Just the world and you.

Your thoughts are heard
But there are no words
To hide behind
And all you see is who you want to be.

Well I've been down that road before.
It's not that easy anymore.
Only you can find
Your smile and your peace of mind.

Someone once told me
That a melody
Could change a person's soul.

Patch up the cracks and get moving along
Because the world's been waiting
For you to come home, step into the light
It's your time to shine,
Look at everybody and say goodbye.

You'll be down that road again,
Never knowing when it will end.
You'll cry, and you'll laugh
And you'll smile,
But remember you'll have a friend
And you'll figure it out in the end.

**Nina Pulimood (14)**

# Expectations

I've been trapped inside my head but I can't express myself,
Keep thinking 'bout all the things I've done,
Been trapped inside so long I don't feel like I'm living,
Just living a lie all along.

I don't want to live up to your expectations,
It's all a test you want me to pass,
Don't make me live up to your expectations,
My life is *mine* so let me be free!
I've been hiding away all my feelings,
But they have to escape somehow,
Been bottled away so long they're forgotten,
But now the bottles are starting to crack

It's time to take what's mine and get out of this place,
Smash the glass of your 'perfect' world,

I'm not gonna live up to your expectations,
Life's not a test, I won't let you judge me,
Don't make me live up to your expectations,
My life is *mine* so I'm running free!

Now I'm rebelling, just you try to forget me,
I'll be a scandal you'll talk of for years,
I'll break all the rules ever laid!

Not gonna live up to your expectations,
Let me leave, I can break my way out.
Don't make me live up to your expectations,
If I can dream then I'll know I'm alive,
Cos if you dream then there's nowhere to hide,
Yeah, if you dream then you know you're alive.

If you dream then you know you're alive.

**Eliza Day (14)**

# Relations

As I stare into your eyes
I struggle to see
The real you
As it's hidden too deep

Yes, your beauty shines out
From your radiance within
And yet I still wonder
How can this not be sin?

For you see, my love
I cannot wait
To see the real you
Or to be your mate

I only want your love
Friends we cannot be
So to you my love
Farewell to thee

But please do not fret
I will be with you inside
You don't even have to look
Just close your eyes

So I say farewell
For I must go
Somewhere far away
Somewhere you can't know

For I can't live a life
With someone so strange
Yet I manage to love -
This is no game.

**Amy Frith (13)**

# Walk Away

I never thought that I could be so wrong
The lies that you kept feeding me
Thinking that it would go on and on
I feel betrayed
I feel so afraid
I feel like our love can't carry on

But then you tell me that you love me
Like it comes from the heart
You tell me that you need me
And we'll never fall apart
But now I know the truth
About you, and I say
It's time for me
To walk away

You try to email me and ring my phone
I try to ignore you
But now you're coming round
To my home
I feel betrayed
I feel so afraid
I feel like our love can't carry on

But then you tell me that you love me
Like it comes from the heart
You tell me that you need me
And we'll never fall apart
But now I know the truth
About you, and I say
It's time for me
To walk away.

**Rhea Milson (13)**

# Save Me From The Night

Where are the lights that lead us to love?
Where are the angels up above?
When we are having a happy day,
Why do the blue skies turn to grey?
Or is it just me?

Is there anybody out there who knows what I'm going through?
Won't you come and tell me cos I don't know what to do.
I've lost everything in my life, my soul and my light,
So come and save me,
Save me from the night.

I've walked down these streets a hundred times
But tonight they look different,
And I don't know why.
The moon's shining down, it's getting late
And I just can't wait until morning.

Is there anybody out there who knows what I'm going through?
Won't you come and tell me cos I don't know what to do.
I've lost everything in my life, my soul and my light,
So come and save me,
Save me from the night.

And I don't know what to do,
It's killing me inside,
I'm still scared and I don't know why.

Is there anybody out there who knows what I'm going through?
Won't you come and tell me cos I don't know what to do.
I've lost everything in my life, my soul and my light,
So come and save me,
Save me from the night.

**Laura Gillingham (13)**

# Lyrics

The first time that we met I knew it all, right then and there,
You were the one for me.
But as the years went on I realised there's no such thing
'Cause we're not meant to be.
No matter what I do or say, you never seem to care
Now what can I believe?
We're fake, we don't have any meaning (please)
I need you to let go of me.

I ask for your forgiveness
'Cause I've already made up my mind
I've had enough of all your lies
I need to try to stop and rewind.

I'm so sorry for running away
But I need to break free from you
I'm so sorry, but I need to live my life
Please, I need you to let go of me.

For all these years I've been too blind to see what we've become
I need my life back now
I wish I could feel the freedom
I need to break our vow.

I ask of your forgiveness
'Cause I've already made up my mind
But all is lost, please, my baby, oh
I have so much to find.

I'm sorry for running away
But I need to break free from you
I'm so sorry, but I need to live my life
Please, I need you to let go of me.

**Rowan McNamee (14)**

# Never Give Up

Every day that you live
there are always chances.
Some you may have to give,
others you're gonna have to take.

Never give up
you're gonna need to finish what you've started
If you just leave all your effort into what you've done
then you may not finish it later on in life
so once you've begun
you must never give up.

You always feel
the urge to give up all the time
So here's the deal . . .
keep tryin' and you gotta chance in life!

Never give up
you're gonna need to finish what you've started
If you just leave all your effort into what you've done
then you may not finish it later on in life
so once you've begun
you must never give up.

Even though some chances can get so frustrating
you gotta keep pushin' until you reach the end!

Never give up
you're gonna need to finish what you've started
If you just leave all your effort into what you've done
then you may not finish it later on in life
so once you've begun
you must never give up.

**Danielle Hatton (12)**

# Young Love Never Dies

So I took everything
Memories from you and me
And put them in a box - I sealed it tight with superglue
And put it where I couldn't reach it
And in 66 years from now I'll walk into a pub
And smell your smell
Walk up as if we'd never met
And start an average conversation
Then we'd laugh and joke just like a house on fire
Walk to the park, sit on the swings, swing higher and higher
And chatter all night long
Until at 9 minutes past 1 you pause . . . and say
'I feel like I've known you my whole life
You make me feel so damn alive'
And I say, 'There's something you ought to know
I cannot tell you but I'll show you.'
Hand in hand running down the cobble streets
Past the place where we used to meet
When we were childhood sweethearts
Through the door and up the stairs
Tiptoes standing on a chair
To reach up for the dusty box
Thrust open the superglue
Pull out the pictures of me and you
From a long, long, long time ago
I don't know what you're going to do
You pull me right up close to you
And it's the way it used to be
I'll never let you go again, because you hold the key
The key that fits my heart.

**Bethany Wadlow (15)**

# Being Alone

You captured my heart
Right from the start,
My feelings just for you,
Then you went away one day
And left me in disarray.
I can't believe it's true.
By myself again,
Yes, I'm all alone again.
The pain I feel,
But it's so unreal
Being all alone again.
Missing you each day,
As my tears run away,
Time alone in my heart,
Now that we're apart.
I cannot go on each day,
Being alone again,
And I thought we were friends
Until you broke my heart again.
I thought we were good together,
Hoping it would last forever,
But times and things change,
As we live our lives in rage,
Breaking our hearts for whatever.
Being alone again,
Wishing you back again,
I miss you each day
In every possible way.
Loving you so much
Just hurts me each day.

**Lisa Berry (12)**

# Going Down

*Are* you ready to be drowned,
Ready to go down, *honey?*
I'm never around,
Always bringing you down,
You're being drowned by me,
Still you won't see,
I'm bringing you down,
Still you don't make a sound,
So *honey*, tell me
*Are* you ready to be drowned,
Ready to go down, *honey?*
You must be getting lonely
In your own company,
You're not ready to be taken under,
I carry round the storm and thunder,
You'd better run away, dear
Before my demons catch up with you,
'Cause there's
Nothing left for you here,
Now *honey,*
*Are* you ready to be drowned,
Ready to go down *lonely.*
Lightning in your side,
With a shock of cyanide,
Say, is that the way you died?
You're being drowned by me.
*Are* you ready to go down,
Ready to go round, *honey?*
Start making a sound,
Start standing your ground.

**Megan Paul (15)**

# Love Is A Roller Coaster Ride

You wanted me to change
To see a different side of the world
You asked me to and I did
I always grant what you ask for
And I never say no because
Love is a roller coaster ride.
Up and down we go
With our arms held high
And the wind blowing in our hair.
Fallouts, kissing,
Is all part of love.
Why, oh why do I always miss out?
I get on the ride, I see your face,
I try to get off but it was too late.
We went up the hill and you took my hand,
I saw the past, the present, then the future.
How can I love you with our past?
Love is a roller coaster ride,
Up and down we go
With our arms held high
And the wind blowing in our hair.
Fallouts, kissing,
Is all part of love.
Why, do I, why do I always miss out?
I need your help, I need to live,
I need, I need you back
Because I love you.
Love is a roller coaster ride,
Up and down we go.
I want it, I want it now.

**Gemma Skipper (13)**

# Who You Are

Listen to the beat of the drums
Listen to the strumming of guitars
It doesn't matter what we want
As long as you understand!
Listen to the beat of your heart
You can't lose it
The beat of your heart
You can use it
No matter how wide or far!
Listen to the beat of your heart
It doesn't matter
If you're on a star
You can use it
It will show you who you are!
Even if you fly away
It will be there
As high a the sky
It's who you are
You can't lose it
Cos it's there for you
When you need it!
The beat of your heart
Just listen to the beat of your heart
As long as you use it
You can't lose it
It's who you are!
Listen to the beat of the drums
Listen to the strumming of guitars
As long as you've got what you need
You will know who you are!

**Eleanor Gregory (13)**

# Carry On

You were always there
I was never scared
You made me feel so safe
Like nothing could harm me
It always reminds me that you care
I feel so invincible
When I sing I feel strong
You bring the voice out in me
Taught me it's OK to let you in
And now you're in my heart, I'm not letting you go
Every day makes me stronger
Every sweat makes it worth it and know I'm not wrong
There's not an ocean I wouldn't swim
A desert I wouldn't cross
Or a song I wouldn't sing for you
The world didn't change me, you did
Now life looks so much better
And the days look so much brighter than before
If you left, you'd leave me with so much strength inside
The heart of a soldier fighting on
And the further I go, our hearts beat as one
These are just words but with a meaning
To show the world and you inside
That this isn't something I can hide
Strength comes from the ones we let in
Just don't give up, keep fighting on
'Cause things right here are goin' strong
I'd never change a minute of us
Time's gonna keep us holding on
I know you'll be there if I need you.

**Abbie-Leigh Allard (15)**

# I First Realised How I Felt

I first realised how I felt
that day you made my heart melt
that made me wanna shout a thousand cries
Of 'I love you sweetheart, I love you honey'
my heart is yours for no amount of money
just to see those eyes would be great
because the first time was no fate
God sent me you to love and to hold
to cherish until my body grows old
have you in my arms, my hands on your cheeks
look into your eyes and feel myself grow weak
then kiss on the forehead, my hand on your heart
tell you I'm sorry for being so far apart
then with all the cries of happiness and joy
knowing that time itself cannot destroy
this precious moment that when U give in
I kiss you deeply, melting my heart within
so passionate and loving that kiss will be
finally we're together, just you and me
and sadly end that kiss after a while
look in your eyes and see you smile
then arms around you I'll whisper in your ear
in a moment so perfect it brings me to tears
I'll say, 'Sweetheart, I love you, you're my world
nothing will make my love for you unfurl,
you're all I want and need, my sweetheart
I'll take your hands still close together
tell you I'm here for you always and forever
I am yours, my darling, you know it's true
Cos I simply am in love with you.

**Matthew Gutteridge (16)**

# Love Letter

Hey Baby, you've got me going crazy
Cos I wanna be more than just friends
We're inseparable but I feel I can't have you
So I'm taking it one day at a time.
I play my music to make me less paranoid
I've got to hold on cos it's a crazy world.
It's six minutes till 7.05, when we met.
I am just an underdog and I'm lovesick.
We are the kids of the future and
Love is on its way for us poor, unfortunate souls.
I'm gonna getcha good cos you're much better
I am what I am and I'm burnin' up
So don't speak and we can play some games.
You're out of this world and a one-man show
Please be mine and put me on a shelf.
Just a little bit longer and we'll be in Year 3000,
Where we'll live to party and bb good
We'll turn right to Australia
Where you'll forget about the pizza girl,
Keep it real and buy a little monkey.
So don't keep pushin' me away
Cos I'm still in love with you.
I'm gonna say goodnight and goodbye
But I'm sorry for saying I didn't love you.
When you said, 'Hello, beautiful,'
You're what I go to school for
And when you look me in the eyes
I feel like a video girl.
But I was wrong again and I didn't appreciate you,
So won't you fly with me?

**Victoria Wilson (13)**

# Foolish

I was too foolish to believe
That you would make me whole again,
I was too foolish to believe
That you were the one for me!
We would always talk about our future,
I thought it was my true love fantasy.
When I woke up in the morning
I used to look at you and smile,
But now I'm alone!
I was too foolish to believe
That you would make me whole again,
I was too foolish to believe
That you were the one for me!
See I don't know why,
I left everything to be with you,
I couldn't see through all the lies,
You made me believe it was something good,
But I guess I was wrong,
I let my feelings get too strong,
I should have left you,
I should never have trusted you!
I was too foolish to believe
That you would make me whole again,
I was too foolish to believe
That you were the one for me!
Oh, I never should have trusted you,
It was a mistake, believe me.
Oh, the fantasy is over,
I should never have trusted you but . . .
I was foolish!

**Briony Willis (13)**

# Never Shoulda Happened

There's some things that never shoulda happened
And it's up to you and the people around you
To make a change for once and for all
There's this one guy I used to know
Forced into a gang
He broke into a house one night
And made a big bang
He used the gun, but then he had to run
Before he got done
And that's a thing that never shoulda happened
And it's up to you and the people around you
To make a change for once and for all
There's this other guy I knew
He was in a gang too
One of the mistakes he made?
Well he carried a blade
Stole it from someone's kitchen
Before gettin' sent straight to prison
That's a thing that never shoulda happened
And it's up to you and the people around you
To make a change for once and for all
Stay off the streets, instead dance to the beats
Of your music, better be quick
If you wanna make that change
Help stop the things that never shoulda happened
Spread the word
Make yourself heard
Stop those things that never shoulda happened
And it's up to you and the people around you
To make a change for once and for all.

**Brooke Bailey (12)**

# You've Stolen My Heart

I've lost something that I really can't replace
And, though they say love will end never,
They really have no idea just how I feel,
Now that you've locked up my heart forever.
Because you've stolen my heart,
Locked it up, lost the key,
And it'll stay by your side for infinity.
Now, I've been to the four corners of the Earth
And I've sailed on the seven seas,
I've crawled through the darkest cavern deep below,
And I've scaled the tallest trees,
Because you've stolen my heart,
Locked it up, lost the key,
And it'll stay by your side for infinity.
Now, I've climbed to the peak of Mount Everest
And I've searched Etna's crater too,
I swam right across the Great Barrier Reef,
And I even checked London Zoo.
Because you've stolen my heart,
Locked it up, lost the key,
And it'll stay by your side for infinity.
Now, I've flown into deepest, darkest space,
And searched every planet I found,
And all I needed, all I wanted to find
Was the heart you stole without a sound.
Because you've stolen my heart,
Locked it up, lost the key,
And it'll stay by your side for infinity,
Because you've stolen my heart,
Locked it up and lost the key.

**Charlotte Parker (14)**

# Waiting

I'm sitting, waiting for the phone to ring,
Biting my nails, rocking to and fro.
Do you care that I'm waiting, waiting?
Or will you leave me at an all-time low?
Waiting, waiting, I spend my life waiting for you,
Bitter disappointment and tears too.
How long will my patience last
Before I end up in a downright mess for you?
I'm all dressed up and ready to go,
Make-up on and hair de-frizzed.
I stand by the door, waiting, waiting,
Thinking of the last time you and me kissed.
Waiting, waiting, I spend my life waiting for you,
Bitter disappointment and tears too.
How long will my patience last
Before I end up in a downright mess for you?
When your phone rings, on our date, baby,
I tell you to leave it, but you say no.
I sit on my own, waiting, waiting,
Why does the time seem to go so slow?
Waiting, waiting, I spend my life waiting for you,
Bitter disappointment and tears too.
How long will my patience last
Before I end up in a downright mess for you?
Why should I wait, why should I?
Everything you do is disappointing,
But you are my life and my loved one,
So I just keep on waiting, waiting,
Waiting, waiting, I spend my life waiting for you.
Waiting, waiting, I spend my life waiting for you, baby.

**Nicola Bowen (13)**

# I Have To Be Strong

When you and me are together
It means the world to me,
Doesn't matter about the weather,
As long as you're here with me.
My heart goes really fast
When I see your face,
I hope this can last,
You make me strong,
I hope our love will last.
I stare at the stars thinking of you,
As the night goes darker
I write, I love you,
With the magic marker you gave me.
I see your face
As I pack my case.
I'm walking out the front door,
My heart is feeling really unsure.
Is it the right thing
That I have done?
I'm starting to feel like I am someone.
You meant the world to me,
But sorry, you used the wrong key,
You messed with me
And look where we are now.
I left the house
Feeling proud of myself.
I can't stand here in this pain,
You think this love is a childish game.
We have been apart so long,
But I have to be strong.

**Jessica Preston (15)**

# Survivors

Smoke, dust, a memory of us
Broken glass fading to black
A stutter, we're choking
We're both left wide open.
Everything we ever knew
Just went up in flames.
Our things, our clothes
Everything we own
In melted photo frames.
We've set our hearts on fire
We lost control and now we're
Fighting like survivors.
Love, hate, are they the same?
Blinked twice and burned again
A ringing, no answer
Our love is a cancer.
Everything we ever knew
Just went up in flames.
Our things, our clothes
Everything we own
In melted photo frames.
We've set our hearts on fire
We lost control and now we're
Fighting like survivors.
We never let anything
Tear us down until
The day, baby, we burned out
Fighting like . . .
Fighting like . . .
Fighting like survivors.

**Becki-Anne Higgins (17)**

# Inspiration

When I look out the window, the first thing that I see:
People walking, cars zooming, colours in the street.
When I turn on the news, the first thing that I hear:
Bombs exploding, guns blazing, civilians living in fear.
When I eat at an average pub, the first thing that I taste:
Overdone or undercooked, it's been prepared in haste.
I could go on, for pages and pages about senses of this Earth,
But I'm afraid not one of those pages would contain any mirth.
So I think I should take it slow, I shall not hurry, rush or race,
Like everyone else, not taking it in, just getting from place to place.
Because people don't really notice that you are in fact, there,
All they see is a mound of flesh, taking up their air.
Always busy, never ready for the days that come ahead,
And my mum wonders why I spend so much time in bed.
It's because I don't want to get caught up in the world's reality,
I guess logic was never really my speciality.
I work more in the realms of dreams, where fantasy and imagination rule,
Though sometimes this beloved dream world can in fact be cruel.
I am, of course, speaking of those horrors in the dark,
Nightmares, lurking in the shadows, silencing the larks.
But then there are no scarier nightmares than the one I live in,
Where just being different, and not a sheep, is some kind of sin.
Stereotypes and archetypes just typing up everywhere,
If you don't look the same as them, they're sure to stop and stare.
I am different, unique, one of a kind, not the same,
This I can confidently state fact, not claim.
But that's because I've stopped and thought, and found just who I am,
But there are those who think that rubbish, that I am just a sham.
To you, I say, I don't really care, this is me and that is you,
And if you don't like it, you just need to get a clue!

**Michelle Stevens (16)**

# Time

Roller skates and bumblebees
Holding hands and grazing knees
Dressing up and falling down
Paul and Mike are coming round
Being good to stay up late
Forget to shut the garden gate
Built a house up in a tree
Been making plans since I was three
Time catches everyone
The world goes round the sun
And the memory lives on in my heart
Skiving French and stealing Mars
Hanging out in Rosie's bar
Getting changed straight after school
Smoking fags and playing pool
Getting caught in someone's car
This time, kid, you've gone too far
Time catches everyone
And the world goes round the sun
And the memory lives on in my heart
Going back to the start forever, forever
Up and down to Donegal
Learning lines to play the fool
Hanging out at Hannah's bar
Got too drunk to drive the car
Even though I'd love to stay
And even though you're now for me
Soon you'll be a memory
Time catches everyone
And the memory lives on in my heart forever.

**Amie Hughes (15)**

# Angel

Come to me, little angel,
Show me your miracle.
There's an angel watching over me,
You have one too, I guarantee.
Let her come forth, be your saviour,
She will help you I'll ensure.
Come to me little angel,
Show me your miracle.
She'll blow away the darkness
And show you the light,
With hands that hold, hands that heal
It may seem surreal.
Come to me, little angel,
Show me your miracle.
Your angel guards your soul,
In a treasure box called her own,
Let her white wings unfold,
They're encrusted with gold.
Come to me, little angel,
Show me your miracle.
She is a supreme being,
And she is all-seeing.
She'll guide you through your fears
And wipe away your tears.
Come to me, little angel,
Show me your miracle.
Her halo will shine,
She's very divine,
Go to her, little angel,
Show her your miracle!

**Kayleigh Woodhouse (13)**

# He Said He Loves Me

He said he loves me
He wouldn't say that if he sees what I see
Talking to other girls like he's not with me
When I saw it I couldn't believe it
An emptiness filled my heart
His faded love tore me apart
All that flashed were the memories
When we first met, sweet talk, jeez
I can't even think about it
I frown every time I rap about it
Can't explore the rest of my brain
It's blocked by a form of anger and rage
It ain't nuttin' though, I'll hide before the rain
Gotta get out of it before I go insane
I know it won't be the same
But it's done now, over
I'm crying on a shoulder
Waiting for God to lift me up again
And help me forget about way back when
I can't look at him like I used to
The love's gone, it's time to move on
He had to do wrong
Couldn't just stay strapped like Trey songs
And can't help but wait
For me and see
That what we had was special
But he couldn't wait
Not for me, anyways
I guess now it's goodbye
Want me back? It's too late.

**Melissa Caton (15)**

# Kisses In The Rain

Somebody forgot to turn out the stars this morning
And make it turn into day
And now I'm holding hands with the darkness
It soothes me anyway
All the memories of us together
Still linger on my mind
From the sweetness of your lips
Described in beauty I can't confide
To the smell of your scarf you gave me
In winter when I was cold
I sit and wonder to myself
If our story has yet been told
I'll write that story, I'll make it unfurl
About one dark-haired guy who gets the girl
If I could wish I would want to
Know her heart and be devoted
Come back in ten years time and
Find our names on the tree where we wrote it
If I could go back in time
I wouldn't change a thing; I'd even keep the tears
So meet me on the moon, my love
And we'll dance and sing and conquer all our fears
Sometimes I forgot to say, 'How much
I needed you to be there when I broke,'
And you would continue every
Unfinished sentence that I spoke
With words of wisdom, words so wise
You earned my love and didn't have to try
But I was too in love with you to realise
That soon we might end up saying goodbye.

**Frankie Watts (16)**

# I Don't Wanna Be Alone

I don't wanna be alone
Why do you have to go
Leaving me so cold?
Wherever I shall go
You will always be in my heart,
Even though you've gone
I am here to stay.
I don't wanna be alone.
Tears can't express the way I feel
I'm in a lonely place,
Where nothing feels real.
I can see you floating in the air
Like an angel passing by.
The sun becomes dull
As the clouds go by.
I don't wanna be alone.
Why did you have to go?
My world turning bitter,
Everywhere I go,
Why do you have to go?
The world always seems to crash down,
Can't it end like a fairy tale?
Whoa, oh . . .
I don't wanna be alone.
Why do you have to go,
Leaving me so cold,
Wherever I shall go?
Hmmm . . .
Ooo . . .
Yeah!

**Dalveen Bird (15)**

# Can't Let Myself Forget

Last night came quickly,
It always does when I'm alone,
Cos it's the time I think of you.
I thought of all the times
We walked hand in hand,
Strolled along the beach,
Sand beneath our feet.
It's all a memory:
A sad, small memory, but at least it's there.
I saw your face last week when I walked alone, that night;
Unbroken waves and lingering thoughts,
That's where it all began, twilight on the beach.
Tears shine like the stars, the ones we used to watch,
But it doesn't matter now,
Your love's lost all feelings, though.
Unrequited, but still hanging on.
I wear my heart on my sleeve, hope you come back.
Never forget that day you left,
But I won't get back all those tears I cried.
Wasted time on you, I know I deserve better,
You're so far gone, you're like a dream,
More of a nightmare.
Swear I'll not forget you,
I don't want to forget you, you made those days
The happiest days I've had.
I'll never feel that again
Cos you made my life for me,
And you only get one shot, and when I did,
You were right there with me.
You're still here with me.

**Aisling Napier (17)**

# Why The Wait?

They're queuing outside the record shop
The police are hanging around
I go up to the front of the crowd,
I ask them, 'Why the wait?'
They tell me just to get in line
But what for? What for?
What are we waiting for? What are we waiting for?
Does no one know and do they care?
What are we waiting for? What are we waiting for?
The fact that we're denied the truth is not fair.
I'm fed up of the lies,
I just want the truth,
It's not a lot to ask for.
So give me what I want,
I'm getting desperate,
So give me it now. Now!
What are we waiting for? What are we waiting for?
Does no one know and do they care?
What are we waiting for? What are we waiting for?
The fact that we're denied the truth is not fair.
These endless repeats
They are boring me,
I've seen it all before
And I don't want to see it again.
Why can't there be something different,
Because I want something new, new!
What are we waiting for? What are we waiting for?
Does no one know and do they care?
What are we waiting for? What are we waiting for?
The fact that we're denied the truth is not fair.

**Kieran Sefton (14)**

# What Is Love?

Is love feeling whole inside?
Is love feeling like you never need to cry?
Is love never wanting anything than who's by your side?
Is love an aching that never shows through your eyes?
Is love just a fascination of the mind?
Is love a fire that burns deep inside?
Is love a rose, soft and gentle?
Is love passion, like a dark red rose petal?
Is love a disturbed form of hate
Distorting our minds and messing with our fate?
Is love fragile like an opening and closing gate?
Is love thinking two hearts will never stop on a certain date?
Is love a blissful moment of serenity
Screaming away all our fears,
Holding us dear
Into eternity?
Is it guiding us through each year?
Is love never letting go and always letting our feelings show?
Does it mean we don't have to say no
To the one who never brings you down low?
Is love that never-ending emotion
That's as strong as the first time you kissed,
Echoing through each minute . . .
Will the first touch ever be missed?
Is it shared between two innocent hearts of lovers?
Are they just walking through the paths of life
To be discovered or re-light the fire
Of the deep connection that may have got lost
In the hope that the burning, soft sunlight
Will melt the cold, hard frost . . . ?

**Jane Clegg (16)**

# Isolated

All I can see is a wall in front of me
On the wall are blocked-out windows
Out there is so much to do
So much to see
With my fantasy, yeah, yeah, yeah
That's for me to know
And for you to find out
All the secrets lying out there
Just want to escape

I just wanna escape, I just wanna leave
I just wanna get out of this box
Why can't you see that you're trapping me
In this claustrophobic box?
I wanna see the world
For my fantasy
Instead of being hooked up in here
I, I wanna get away, to my sanctuary
For my lovely sweet escape
I'm isolated, isolated, isolated

You got me whizzed up in here
So trapped I find it hard to breathe, yeah
I find it hard to communicate
With the outside world today!
Today, today, today
I'm gonna break free
I'm gonna get these chains off me
Gonna smash the wall
Break it down
Cos I feel isolated!

**Jordan Hutchinson (14)**

# Thank Goodness For Technology

Been waiting on my balcony all day,
Waiting for you to come and say
My princess come and let down the ladder of love,
But Dad won't let me outdoors, you see,
And I cannot get you to be with me,
Thank goodness for the invention of technology.

Facebook, Bebo, MSN,
Twitter, T-Mobile, IM,
Email and the internet -
Is exactly how we met!

Call me at about quarter to seven
And we'll talk until about half-past eleven
Cos that's when I run out of minutes
The way you did last night talking to me
Sign in after on MSN
And we'll have a conversation by IM
We'll be sensible on the webcam
And talk for as long as we can.

Cinderella was unlucky, she had no cell
I'm guessing that's what happened to Ariel
They couldn't call their heroes to come and set them free
I'm happy that this is no fairytale story
Or how would we ever be you and me?
Give a round of applause to Wi-Fi connection, baby!

Facebook, Bebo, MSN,
Twitter, T-Mobile, IM,
Email and the internet -
Is exactly how we met!

**Rachel Ogunkoya (14)**

# Break My Heart

I feel like this is falling apart
I don't like the distance between me and you
Is this what you want?
We can run
Run away from the fights
'Cause that's all we seem to do lately
And I don't wanna fight with you

The way you look at me says so much
The walls came crashing down
I just want to avoid the fights
Maybe it's just me
Maybe my heart wants to break
So break, break, break my heart
Yeah, break, break, break my heart
Why not break, break, break my heart?

There's so much you need to know
I wish I could see how badly this will hurt
When you say goodbye
So I can try to stay away
You're driving me crazy

The way you look at me says so much
The walls came crashing down
I just want to avoid the fights
Maybe it's just me
Maybe my heart wants to break
So break, break, break my heart
Yeah, break, break, break my heart
Why not break, break, break my heart?

**Vicky Woodford (16)**

# Strength

She's been to eighteen funerals
But that isn't gonna ruin her day.
Gets dressed and goes to school
Acting like everything is okay.
Could you tell, if you saw her eyes?
If she laughed, would you feel her pain?
Her broken smile hides the grief inside
But she won't let it leave a stain.

Strength isn't being able to feel no emotion or hurt,
Strength isn't being able to make it better from the worse . . .
It's standing up
And it's speaking out
And it's saying, 'Forget the day I had',
It's better off thinking
That this is just living
And no day's a waste if you've still got a smile on your face.

He bought her a diamond ring,
Words of love slipping through his lips,
It was their last anniversary,
He never got to say his proposal script,
Could you tell if you saw his grin?
Would you have heard lies if he'd spoken?
A small felt box thrown into the bin,
The only clue that his heart was broken.

Strength isn't what you think -
It's standing in quicksand refusing to sink . . .
It's building a chain with too few links . . .
Strength.

**Cordelia Chui (14)**

# The Girl With No Name

Do I need to touch you,
To leave a piece of me with you?
Tattoo my name across your heart
To finally really get through?
Absence makes the heart grow fonder,
How much more can one heart take?
Your ways, they leave me hypnotised,
From this spell I cannot break

Do you even see me,
Will there ever be a cure?
Ever, forever running, never getting closer to your door.
Do you ever see me standing outside your windowpane?
Look into my eyes, reach into your heart and see
The girl with no name.

Feels like I'm screaming, shouting,
Trying to get through to you.
I'm fighting this fight alone.
What else can I possibly do?
Your face, your smell, your touch,
It almost feels like you really mean too much to me.
Gotta break outta this imprisonment
So you can be mine and we can be free.

Do you even see me,
Will there ever be a cure?
Ever, forever running, never getting closer to your door.
Do you ever see me standing outside your windowpane?
Look into my eyes, reach into your heart and see
The girl with no name.

**Rebecca Baker (16)**

# Picture Perfect

So many memories we shared together
So many good times between us
I got that picture set as my wallpaper
It makes me smile every time I look at it,
And it captured the untouchable moment
And it brings back that feeling that we both felt.

Those magical moments will stay in our hearts forever.
We capture those memories and we share our dreams together.
Everything's flawless, everything's unmissable,
Everything . . . picture perfect.

The times we spent together glow in the wooden frame,
It makes me think of all the wonderful things that you are.
And you shine so bright, you're my winning star in the night,
An we connect our thoughts and feelings,
Make them last with that priceless picture.

Those magical moments will stay in our hearts forever.
We capture those memories and we share our dreams together.
Everything's flawless, everything's unmissable,
Everything . . . picture perfect.

And I stick those pictures in my scrapbook
And they'll stick in my heart,
And we'll never let go of those indescribable and incredible moments
I just can't hold back.

Those magical moments will stay in our hearts forever.
We capture those memories and we share our dreams together.
Everything's flawless, everything's unmissable,
Everything . . . picture perfect.

**Cathy Madden (15)**

# From The Start

Tell me when will this story end,
It must be nearly done,
Don't leave me on a cliffhanger,
Cos I'll still be holding on.
I feel empty inside,
Nowhere to run, nowhere to hide.
The pain cuts through me like a knife,
I've never felt like this in all my life.
You said let's try,
But I guess you changed your mind
Cos you did nothing
And neither did I,
So we fell apart
And you broke my heart
From the very start.
Never felt this way before,
Don't think I can take it anymore,
But I just can't walk away,
My heart's aching, breaking, so sore.
The way you smiled,
The way your eyes shone,
The way they looked into mine,
All the words you used to say,
Are gone with the wind,
Never to be heard again.
And as the curtain's closing,
I take my final bow,
I think I understand
This story's over now.

**Rachel Williamson (14)**

# Just Listen To Me!

When I was little you used to care
But now I'm older you don't understand
All the things I'm going through.
The only person I can trust is you
Because no one listens to my voice.
Just listen to me,
My voice is never heard
Over all this stress.
Mum, you're the only one who listens.
My friends talk about all this gossip
Which I don't understand,
They talk this music rubbish
And their favourite male singer,
As you know, it's not my fave thing.
Just listen to me,
My voice is never heard
Over all this stress.
Mum, you're the only one who listens.
I may seem like the girl you feel sorry for
But I'm a lot like you.
After the story I sung in class
They all seem to listen now.
Will you give me a chance to sing this song to you?
Then finally you may understand me.
Just listen to me,
My voice is never heard
Over all this stress.
Mum, you're the only one who listens,
Now hear my cry.

**Danni Evans (12) & Amber Turner (13)**

# Did It Have To End Like This?

It only started yesterday!
Was that the final kiss?
And then you went away,
What was wrong with me?
What was wrong with us?
Did you really have to go?
Was it not enough
That you had my love?
How could you ever be so low?
Guess my love for you is still strong!
Now alone, what shall I do?
Should I just move on
Or should I stick with you?
What as wrong with me?
What was wrong with us?
Did you really have to go
Was it not enough
That you had my love?
How could you ever be so low?
I suppose this is the end!
My future's looking down!
No hope for me at all!
And my heart is hurting now!
I know what went wrong with me!
And what went wrong with us!
And it as best for us to part!
You always had my love,
But it proved not enough.
Yes, you hurt me from the start!

**Katiey Vine (14)**

# Fly Away

I'm just the kind of girl
That was so shy,
I looked at the sparkles in my eyes
And thought to myself
I'm ready to do this,
Don't care what they say,
I'm ready to fly away
To a better place.
I'm ready to show myself
To the world,
Just lift up my wings and fly away,
Fly away.
I'm standing here
Looking at myself,
I want to show the world
What I can do and see
And what I want to know.
If I'm that girl
That will fly away
To a better place
I'm ready to fly away
To a better place.
I'm ready to show myself
To the world,
Just lift up my wings
And fly away,
Fly away,
Fly away,
Fly away . . .

**Mai Wilson (10)**

# Get Your Time

You wanna live the life you never could,
Do the things your mama said you never should,
Jump up and get down
And kick off and scream out.
Well baby, there ain't no one goin' to stop you now!
'Cause it's time,
It's your time to let go.
Yeah, it's time,
Your time to lose control.
No one ever said it,
But you know you won't regret it,
So go ahead and get it . . .
Get your time.
Now you can do this thing the easy way, you know,
Just pack a couple of bags and let's go.
We can make it together,
But baby, it's now or never . . .
'Cause I ain't goin' to wait forever.
'Cause it's time,
Your time to get away.
Yeah, it's time
To make it your own way.
No one ever said it
But you know you won't regret it,
So go ahead and get it . . .
Get your time.
Jump up and get down
And kick off and scream out,
You know you've got to get your time!

**Natalie Tomlinson (16)**

**109**

# Why Do We Cry?

At a young age people in my family died
But I only felt one, you saw it in my eyes
Since then I've always been known as down to ride
Not another family member, don't want to say 'bye
And when you find out, first thing you do is cry
So I ain't got no more tears and it ain't no lie
All these bars I put my heart in, I'll tell you why
Cos I don't want to see another family member die
It's a hard life that we're living in
Why you rising up your knife and killing him?
You should know better, you should be listening
Because it's peer pressure and you're just giving in
Listen to the positive bars that I'm givin' in
And tell your friend it hurts when you stick it in
Don't you think life would be better glistening
And it's annoying when you turn on the TV
Because all you get is people committing crimes, see
You see everyday guys getting shot
Talking big because he's got a Glock
Take a knife, stabbing everyone around
Get shot and man drop to the ground
I know a little boy who died at nine
Just because a wasteman's holding a knife
The Bible says don't let pride fool you
But that's what you done by shooting another youth
It's life or death and I choose life
How do you believe it's alright
To walk around with guns and knives?
And now he's gone where the sun don't shine.

**Kwesi Mensah (12)**

# Street Talk

If you're on the streets or in the court
It's a guarantee you will be judged by the way you talk
The way you walk
It doesn't really matter if you're tall or short
'Cause if you don't follow the rules of street talk
You might get jumped on your own sidewalk
Teenagers these days are the new generation
If you don't have mates it can cause complication
Walking alone you feel the hesitation
Scared of the teenagers at the train station
Drinking cider and probably takin'
What type of world are these kids creatin'?
My name is Jack and I'm only 14
Growing up fast and becoming a teen
I like to sit around and joke with my mates
But I don't go around punching people in the face
I don't do drugs but I have in the past
Because of the weed it increased my dyslexia
Also leavin' me with permanent schizophrenia
Takin' drugs ruined my mental health
But it made me realise I wasn't myself
It don't make you cool and it don't give you wealth
If anything, man, it ruins your life
Pretty soon you will realise the effects are tight
Like being ignored by the people you like
So if you're offered to smoke some dope
It's one little word, just say nope
Now I'm done I keep myself to myself
Don't be the cool kid, just be yourself.

**Jack Collier (14)**

# Blinded By Love

I was looking, but not really seeing
What was right in front of me.
It's too late for reality.
Stuck in this fantasy,
You hide behind masks
Of who you are and
Who you want to be.
I thought there was a connection,
Me and the fake you.
I never believed in love at first sight
Until I met you.
You were everything a girl would want,
Her very own Prince Charming.
I gave you my heart
But you shattered it.
I'm left with the remains,
All because I was a fool,
To be blinded by love.
The man I fell in love with
Is still somewhere inside,
But I'm done waiting for him.
It's like waiting for rain in the desert -
Useless, hopeless, disappointing -
So I'll move on
And you'll be sorry you waited
For the rain.
And I'll say, 'Too late, I'm over you.'
I can see clearly now,
No longer blinded by love.

**Catherine Abe (16)**

# The Never-Ending Pain

I'm gonna turn insane,
I can't take the pain
Any longer;

My body's aching
From my head down to my toes.

I've had the pain
More than a year,
I need to cure the pain
Or I'll have it
Another year.

I'm gonna turn insane,
I can't take the pain
Any longer;

My body's aching,
More, more and more.

I've had the pain
More than a year,
I need to cure the pain
Or I'll have it
Another year.

I'm gonna turn insane,
I can't take the pain
Any longer.

I'm gonna turn insane,
I can't take the pain
Any longer.

**Lucy Turpin (11)**

# Denial Of Love

I don't need you anymore
I don't want you knockin' at my door
I don't love you, so get it through your head

You hurt me
You broke me
You tore my heart in two
You saved me
Then you left me
When I loved you
When I loved you

We were perfect, you 'n' me
Hand in hand walkin' down the beach
It all changed suddenly
You were acting stranger and stranger
Avoidin' my calls
And when I came around
You wouldn't let me in the house
The day you told me you met someone else

You hurt me
You broke me
You tore my heart in two
You saved me
Then you left me
When I loved you
When I loved you

And no matter what you do
I still love you.

**Laura Alderson (17)**

# Déjà-Vu

Here I am again,
Sat by the pone
Just waiting for your call.
I have seen this before,
You always seem to make me . . .
Fall!

It's déjà-vu,
It happens over and over,
I know what's coming next,
My heart goes colder.
Then I see you in my eyes
And I see me in your arms,
It repeats itself again,
It's déjà-vu.

I'm going in circles
But my head says let him go,
But my heart says no.
I don't know what to do,
I feel stuck with you.

It's déjà-vu,
It happens over and over,
I know what's coming next,
My heart goes colder,
I fall for you again.
My broken heart fades
Then it happens again.
It's déjà-vu.

**Rhiannon Thornton (13)**

# Why?

It's over, it's done
All the worries and the fun
Say sorry, make it right
For all those things you did last night

You looked up when I was fallin'
You looked down when I was callin'
You didn't let me say the word I wanted to
You just left me here lyin'
Rollin' and cryin'
You didn't let me say the word I wanted to
Why?

Whatever you decide
Whatever, I'll fight
All I want is to make this right
My heart is beatin' for you
My heart is beatin' for you
Jumpin' to conclusions
Assumin', arguin', shoutin'
Ending up in tears
Soon I'll end up pouting . . .

You looked up when I was fallin'
You looked down when I was callin'
You didn't let me say the word I wanted to
You just left me here lyin'
Rollin' and cryin'
You didn't let me say the word I wanted to
Why?

**Monica Watt (13)**

# I'm On The Other Side Of The Phone

The future calls us in different directions,
Our fates are different too.
Our destinies lie in different places,
But I am here for you.
When the nightmares get too much
And you just want a place to hide,
Pick up the phone, you know I'm there
On the other side.

I'm here for you
Through sun and rain,
Believe in me, I got your back,
I'll never let them cause you pain.
If the world all turns against you
And you think you're all alone,
Dial my number and press call,
I'm on the other side of the phone.

Other people will come and go,
The odd argument we'll see,
But no one can replace you,
You'll always be the best to me.
Don't be scared, I'm here for you,
Don't think you're all alone,
My voice is always waiting for you
On the other side of the phone.

I'm here for you through sun and rain,
Dial my number, press call again,
I'm on the other side of the phone.

**Rosie Morris (14)**

# Everyday Ordinary Girl

She's an ordinary girl
walking down the street
singin' along to the tune playin' in her ears
bass line pounds as the lights spin around
she's not as ordinary as she appears
for when night falls

She's a rock star
slammin' out riffs on her guitar
jammin' in the underground rock fest
This girl knows  what she is doing
screaming her lungs out to the beat of rock and roll
goin' . . .

Woah, wahey, never let the days fade
Woah, wahey, always seize the day
never let the moments pass you by
make sure you always try
don't let the music stop
strike a chord now
you know what to do
so everybody stamp your feet
and bring it back now.

Up on stage she's a lunatic
at the park she's just a boarder doing kickflips
Doin' stage dives and riding verticals
she's a dreamer livin' out her dream
but to most of the world
she's an everyday ordinary girl.

**Charlotte Bird (14)**

# You're Too Good For Me

Every day is another day-ay,
All my mind does is think about you,
And you think I can wai-ait,
'Cause you know that's all I want to do,
So I can be with you.

And when I see you and you see me,
All you do is walk on by,
As if I am so invisible,
But why-hy do you do that?
'Cause you know I am waiting for you.

And when we text and email
You say that you're too good for me.
When I say I love you, all you say is
You're too good for me, you're too good for me.

When I see you on webcam I look at you and smile,
And your name just goes through my head,
I am so not good enough for you,
I am so not good enough for you.

And when we text and email
You say that you're too good for me.
When I say I love you, all you say is
You're too good for me, you're too good for me.

I love you, I love you so much,
But ever since we last talked on the phone,
You've never replied to my emails or texts,
And I am beginning to wonder, will I ever see you again?

**Sheree Farrant (12)**

# Sarah Louise

You'll always be the one to give me advice,
The one that doesn't mind if I ask her twice.
But this time I swear it'll be the last
'Cause I can tell that Emily's fading fast.

So I plead: Sarah Louise, I don't think I can do this one alone,
So please, can you help me to believe?
Sarah Louise, she's the one I want, but can't retrieve,
Oh Louise, do you think that there's a chance for her and me?

I'll always remember what you said,
You told me never follow your heart, follow your head.
But I swear there's one thing you've overlooked,
Like I'm not good enough for her, and we're not living in a book.

But Sarah Louise, I don't think I can do this one alone,
So please, can you help me to believe?
Oh Sarah Louise, she's the one I want, but can't retrieve,
Oh Louise, do you think that there's a chance for her and me?

I know you told me, 'Boy, you've gotta find your wings and
fly away,'
But I can't leave, no I can't leave without you, oh.
'Cause Sarah, without you how am I ever gonna tell her that I . . .
I love her?
I love her.

Oh Sarah Louise, I don't think I can do this one alone,
So please, can you help me to believe?
Sarah Louise, she's the one I want, but can't retrieve.
Oh Louise, do you think that there's a chance for her and me?

**William Moore (18)**

# The Reasoning

Looking up at the stars
I know you're the one for me,
Naming each star, as to why I love you.
But I find myself unstuck
As I run out of stars for you.
Never let our love go
That flows between you and me.
As the days pass by
The stars begin to fall.
Did you let our love go?
Please just tell me so . . .
I can deal with heartbreak,
I've had it times before, it's my illness,
My only weakness.
How did you know you could get to me like this?
I know you tried your best
Not to hurt me, but it failed like the rest.
I will still hold my head high,
As I dance with falling stars . . .
Naming each as they go,
Filled with the love that is left.
I trusted you so much
But again, you failed me like the rest.
Now the time has come for us to say goodbye.
One last kiss, goodnight . . . goodnight,
Looking up at the stars.
I was wrong about you,
Naming each star, as to why I still love you.

**Kirstey Davis (15)**

# How I Changed My Life

Sitting doing nothing day by day,
Doing nothing, what can I say?
I really need to get out more,
Like sitting on the beach by the shore.
Listening to music, the Kings of Leon,
Going on rides I like to be on.
Hanging with my mates and having a laugh,
When I get dirty, I'll have a bath.
Doing so much gave me a life,
Cutting my sandwich with a knife.
Playing rugby is good for my health,
Unlike a fox, I've got no stealth.
I'm pretty good at maths and alright at art,
I like going racing in my go-kart.
At school like being in drama,
Cos all I think of is, who's the Dalai Lama?
I used to sleep all of the day,
But my body was starting to decay.
This wasn't good for me
Now I've set myself free.
Sitting doing nothing was making me fat,
Now it's clear to me that . . .
I've made a mistake in my life.
If I don't change, I'll never get a wife.
Doing lots of sport is making me fit,
So when I find it hard, I'll never quit.
I've turned my life around,
Look at all the new friends I've found.

**Dan Holmes (13)**

# Karma

What goes around comes around
Humiliation and despair
What I associate this with is the heart about to tear
It's not clear and just there
If only it could be
Maybe I could beat the game of karma and the rules that
                                                    encircle me
A sap I'm being played for, yet I can't force my way free
But you must look me in the eye and see greatly the remorse
And hear me out somewhat so I don't need to use force
I don't want to be at the point of having to change course
But if I don't get the chance to prove myself
It'll kill myself, forever sedate myself
It's like I'm making a fool of myself
But you must have that voice deep inside, saying I'm a genuine lad
Who would do anything for you to atone for what I've done
                                                    that's bad
I seek for forgiveness and a sign with sense of direction
Such as in biblical days with the Lord's resurrection
It's only down to you, you're the key to my redemption
God knows I want nothing more than to be with you and that
But don't drag the point out of it and make me look all bad
I've been humiliated many a time before
I won't accept it anymore
Therefore to denounce me will be something I'll make you pay
                                                    for evermore
I ask to be taken seriously and abandon this game of karma
I acknowledge your perspective and all I want is no more drama.

**Phil McFarland (17)**

# Father's Hand

Alone
Drifting, wild
Like a ship tossed on an ocean
I was a homeless child
Nowhere to go
I couldn't understand
How you could love me so.
Broken
Shattered dreams
In a web, threads I've woven
What does it all mean?
No place to rest
I couldn't understand
Why you'd give me your best.
Hope
Expecting love
Can I feel, a thing so simple?
Peace shaped like a dove
No heart to give
I couldn't understand
Why you would let me live.
Love
Lifted high
In your arms, safe, I am forgiven
You have heard my heart cry
No more sinking sand
Now I understand
Why we need a father's hand.

**Victoria Gault**

# You

I'm so cold
It's like a winter's morning.
I've got a pain,
It feels like burning.
I've got this feeling
Of emptiness.
It's like a hole,
A black hole,
Because when I'm with you
I can touch the sky.
When I'm with you
I will always try.
When I'm with you
I'll always be okay.
When I'm with you
I can almost fly.
When I'm with you
I will never die.
When I'm with you,
Nothing is the same.
So, I'm still cold,
But it's a summer's morning.
I've still got this pain
That feels like burning,
I've got this feeling
When I'm not with you,
And it's like a hole,
A black hole.

**Heather Steele (12)**

# Were You The One?

Why? Why? Oh Why?
That's all I ask myself.
Why? Why? Oh Why?
Do the pieces not fit anymore?
Oh, oh, why? Why did you leave me?
Leave me here, all alone.

All these years I have waited,
All these years I have felt
That you were the one,
The only one right for me.

As I waited at the door for you to come,
My heart was softly dying.
When you didn't turn up,
I just knelt down and I cried.
Oh, you screwed with my heart,
Made me lose my faith
In what is right!
How could I ever forgive you?

All these years I have waited.
All these years I have felt
That you were the one,
The one, right for me.

But now I see,
I see the true story
That shines,
It shines through me!

**Bethany Smart (14)**

# Entourage

You smile at me,
All pretty faces and mocking eyes,
You know that's just the kind of thing
That I despise . . .

C'mon, what's with the entourage,
And what's behind the huge façade?
Just take off the mask,
Is that too much to ask?

I'd give anything to see you fall,
To drag you from your shopping mall,
With your quiet laugh and snide remark,
You think I'm forever in the dark . . .

C'mon, what's with the entourage,
And what's behind the huge façade?
Just take off the mask,
Is that too much to ask?

What I wouldn't do to get inside your head,
And make you see the consequence of everything you said.
You slide the knife, straight in my back,
Spread rumours about everything I lack . . .

C'mon, what's with the entourage,
And what's behind the huge façade?
Just take off the mask,
Is that too much to ask?

C'mon, what's with the entourage . . . ?

**Eve McGlynn (12)**

# Fillin' Me Floor

I can hear the disco music calling me to come
So I'm gonna dance till my feet go numb

So c'mon ladies, I'll show you how to have some fun
The rhythm is ringing in the air
And the dance floor is my lair

The baseline kicks in my adrenalin
The music makes me wanna spin
I have no fear
Now take it up a gear

Now everyone has entered my scene
Feel the beat and you'll know what I mean
So I'm gonna show you my move
Listen to the sound and get down in the groove

The baseline kicks in my adrenalin
The music makes me wanna spin
And there is now a disco ball
The flashing lights fill the hall

Everyone is starting to sweat
My target soon will be met
People creating their own steps
In time your feet will get

The baseline kicks in my adrenalin
The music makes me wanna spin
I'm starting to lose my speech
My mission I will reach.

**Kayne McMillan (14)**

# Untitled

Papa, you sat me on your knee
You told me this was how it's gonna be
I was only young, I thought you were on holiday
But then I realised that you had gone to stay

Mama, bless her, she was on her knees
Crying with only me to comfort her
I tried my best to help, but there really was no need
Cos Papa, it was you that made her bleed

I feel so lonely at night
Your mug still stands where it always was
I hear the sobs all night coming from her lonely bed
She needs someone to dry them away

Mama, bless her, she was on her knees
Crying with only me to comfort her
I tried my best to help, but there really was no need
Cos Papa, it was you that made her bleed

You'll never walk me down the aisle
You'll never see my face when I have my first dance
You'll always be in my heart but not top of my list
Cos you left, oh left me, yeah, you did

Mama, bless her, she was on her knees
Crying with only me to comfort her
I tried my best to help, but there really was no need
Cos Papa, it was you that made her bleed

An apology, Papa, is what I really need.

**Olivia Laxton (15)**

# Unmistakable Love

I couldn't imagine you not there
We'll always share everything we have
Loving you makes my life worth living
Our love is the greatest of all time
It will be a never-ending romance
Unmistakable love

When we're together
We feel safe and secure
When we're together
We can't wish for no more
This can only mean
Unmistakable love
Unmistakable love

I feel lonely when you're not around
You're the only person I desire
I'm never gonna let you go
There ain't nobody better than you
When times are rough, you're always there
Unmistakable love

When we're together
We feel safe and secure
When we're together
We can't wish for no more
This can only mean
Unmistakable love
Unmistakable love.

**Shannon Davies (14)**

# Broken Dreams

It was hard at first
It broke my heart
And though the memories still haunt me
I see it now
It was just never meant to be

Well, I survived a heartbreak
And I survived the memories
I survived the hard times
And now
I'm living on broken dreams
Dreams

The love you gave me
It could drive me crazy
I try my hardest
Not to let it show

Well, I survived a heartbreak
And I survived the memories
I survived the hard times
And now
I'm living on broken dreams
I'm living, I'm living
You've broken my heart
I'm living, I'm living
You've torn me apart
I'm living, I'm living
I'm living on broken dreams.

**Alyx Murray (12)**

# If I Could Go Back I'd Make It Better

Once again. Another failed relationship.
I just couldn't seem to work it.
Maybe it wasn't meant to be?
That was the end.
I can't believe I just shrugged it off and smiled.
You were my everything and I was yours.
I can't believe I was so foolish and let you slip away.

And I swear if I could go back, I'd make it all better
Fix all the wrongs and make them right.
Talk to you every day.
I promise. Just give me one more chance.

I love you. I thought I'd gotten over you
Well I couldn't have been more wrong.
Now you can't be less interested.
I know it now. I promise it'll be better, I just know.
But I just do not know how to tell you,
That baby, I'm in love with you so much
And it is hurting bad.

And I swear, if I could go back, I'd make it all better
Fix all the wrong and make them right.
Talk to you every day.
I promise. Just give me one more chance.
And I swear, if I could go back, I'd make it all better
Fix all the wrong and make them right.
Talk to you every day.
I promise. Just give me one more chance. One more chance.

**Larissa Evans (13)**

# Betrayal

Fists curl, but my nails are digging into my palm
not that the tiny amount of pain makes a difference.
Fists uncurl, just looking at the face I used to smile at
makes me want to strike out at the face I despise.
Fists curl, but would violence solve anything?
I can't afford irrationality right now.
Fists uncurl, but violence would solve a lot.
Everyone staring at me doesn't help.

Mouth opens, but conversing with her repulses me.
How could she say those things? Weren't we friends?
Mouth shuts, but all I want is to scream at her,
'I loved him, and you knew, you cheated us both.'
Mouth opens, but I've nothing to say.
She, who knowingly tormented me, she already knows.
Mouth shuts, but I still want to talk to her.
Despite reasons to stay, I walk away.

I walk away from the corrupt, malevolent creature
who ripped up my life and left me to pick up the pieces
as her perfidy continues to strangle me.
I shut the door on our gawking audience
who scrutinised with their snobbery delight
and she smiled as it was confirmed: she won.

Isn't it funny how the ones who say
'I'll never hurt you,'
Are the ones who hurt you most.
Hilarious.

**Emily Upson (13)**

# Mistaken And Misread

Love can be mistaken and misread
And can leave you better off dead
But there is always a way out
Just never give in to doubt
No matter what you think
That boat will never seem to sink

You have to think before you realise
Don't think you can just make up your mind
Don't think you can love me and leave me
'Cause I won't be another girl you left behind
That might have worked in the past
But now those things are different
Who said we were meant to last?

It makes me sad when I think of our history
Although I will cherish your dear memory
My heart is like a battle ground
When no one else is found
How many tears I cried over you
Any idea what you put me through?

You have to think before you realise
Don't think you can just make up your mind
Don't think you can love me and leave me
'Cause I won't be another girl you left behind
That might have worked in the past
But now those things are different
Who said we were meant to last?

**Ellouise Wheelwright (14)**

# My Type

I thought what you said was awful . . . but the delivery was kind.
You said you thought she was perfect . . .well if perfect's what you like
I think I should leave now because really, I'm not your type.

All the while you talk about your life just makes me annoyed.
Wish I could move on and like . . . show everyone what you're like.

I think it's impossible to break my heart,
So the only thing left to corrupt is my mind.
But maybe that's just because I've been broken-hearted
Far too many times.

But now, when I think back to when we last met,
I've changed quite a bit.
Shame you're still pulling off your stupid ways,
And actually you're quite boring, you know.
Like when you talk about getting pissed
And all the girls and getting kissed,
I swear you read it off the same messed up list.

Now you're round my house,
And you've brought along your cheeky smile.
But if you think that will get you anywhere
You'll be waiting a while.
In which way do you plan to break my mind?
Because baby, I'm feeling stronger this time. This time.

I thought what you said was awful . . .but the delivery was kind.
You said you thought she was perfect . . . well if perfect's what you like
I think you should leave now because sweetheart, you're really not my type.

**Aimee Determann (15)**

# Your Song

Ever since you've gone,
I've been thinking 'bout your song.
It's been playing in my mind,
I just can't put you behind.

I know there's someone new.
I know that now we're through.
I just can't forget your song,
Even though I know it's wrong.

For the music is playing in my heart,
And I just can't help singing my own part.
I keep singing the sweet, sweet melody,
For I miss you so much, so much, you see.

Ever since you walked away,
Ever since that sad, sad day.
I have seen you with your bride,
Walking happily outside.

And I know you don't love me,
But my heart will just not see
That your smiling face has gone.
I just can't forget your song.

For the music is playing in my heart,
And I just can't help singing my own part.
I keep singing the sweet, sweet melody,
For I miss you so much, so much, you see,
Yes, I miss you so much, so much, you see.

**Rachel Connell (14)**

# Together

Walking down the street
Counting all the beats
Music running through the mind
Then I see you standing there
My heart begins to beat
Looking at my feet
Hoping you will notice me
You wind me up
You let me down
So I hate you, yes I hate you
You wind me up
You let me down
So I hate you, but I love you
I see you walking down the road
With the lights dimly lit
You may think I hate you but I don't 'cause
You still live in my heart forever
You wind me up
You let me down
So I hate you, yes I hate you
You wind me up
You let me down
So I hate you, but I love you
You wind me up
You let me down
So I hate you
But I love you.

**Deborah Thomas (15)**

# Depression

I lost my best friend to you,
I lost my closest because of you,
Just leave me,
Get out and don't come back.
You took control of my life,
What else are you going to take from me?
You took control of my thoughts,
You stopped me smiling,
You muted my laughter.
What else are you going to take from me?
You took control of my actions,
You make me hurt myself,
Is this really what you want?
This isn't what I need.
I lost the most important person to me,
I lost myself,
Yeah, just to make you happy.
You took control of my life,
What else are you going to take from me?
You took control of my thoughts,
You stopped me smiling,
You muted my laughter,
What else are you going to take from me?
I lost the most important person to me,
Just to make you happy.
This isn't what I need,
It's just not what I need.

**Gemma Pleavin (16)**

# Hold On

Your body's cold,
You're standing there alone,
Your heart beats fast,
You've run away from home.
Did anybody ever tell you why we care?
Did anybody ever tell you we've been there?
Cos you're so much more than they can ever say . . .
So hold on, if you think you're alone,
So hold on, if you think you'll be gone
Cos we'll be comin' down to fetch you,
Cos we're the only ones you know will stand by.
Your soul is broken, you don't know where to hide.
Your momma's cryin', she don't know why you lied.
Did anybody ever tell you why we care?
Did anybody ever tell you we've been there?
Cos you're so much more than they can ever say . . .
So hold on, if you think you're alone,
So hold on, if you think you'll be gone,
Cos we'll be comin' down to fetch you,
Cos we're the only ones you know will stand by.
Please don't go away, we'll be here to stay
And when the times get rough
We know you'll be tough . . .
So hold on, if you think you're alone,
So hold on, if you think you'll be gone,
Cos we'll be comin' down to fetch you,
Cos we're the only ones you know will stand by.

**Rida Amir (12)**

# Before You Go

Why am I searching in circles,
Will there ever be an end?
Will I ever stop searching?
Will I ever find a friend?
Cos at the moment
I feel so small
I feel like crying
Like I've lost it all
My heart feels empty
My body cold
Like I've never stopped searching
Like a riddle unsolved
My options feel short
Like no one's there
Like people are living
Without a care
This saddens my soul
My eternity cold
I've been searching
A riddle unsolved
But life's too short
To drown in sorrow
You need to look ahead
Towards tomorrow
It can only get better . . . oh
So please help me . . . help me
Before you go.

**Emma Wells (13)**

# How To Fly A Bird

Have you ever had a hobby?
Ohhh.
Have you ever had a choice?
Ohhh.
Maybe it's singing
Or maybe it's dancing,
Ohhh.
But you never had a hobby like me,
You see I know how, how, how
To fly a bird.
Well I learned when I was young,
My best mate was a blue tit
And he came one day,
Gave me a choice,
Said, 'Follow these sheep or
You make your own, own,'
And I'm sure he put a spell on me
Cos I opened my eyes to see an explanation.
Isn't it funny, isn't it weird
On how to fly a bird.
Ohhh, how to fly a bird.
Well my mum said,
'Go for your dreams,'
But I know how to do something
I bet you don't.
Ohh, I know how to fly a bird,
Yeah, how to fly a bird!

**Laila Jones (12)**

# Untitled

The boy was on his own,
He tried to fight through the pain,
A light shone through the window
But he had seen it too many times,
So he just ignored it.
No one knew about the pain,
Oh, the tough, tough pain,
The darkness was tough,
The light hurt his eyes
But he kept going strong.
No one knew where he was,
The police had given up hope,
But the people's hope was oh so strong,
He was always in their hearts.
Twenty years from now
They did not know
They would find him once again,
But something,
Something,
Something was wrong.
He lay by a cross,
Still as a rock.
The whole world cried for him,
They now knew pain,
The horrible pain
This lonely boy
Had been through.

**Samantha Graham (12)**

# Fairy-Tale Life

Once upon a time
In a land far away
The lowly servant girl
Woke to the dawning of the day.
She had a hard run
Filled with tears and laughter
But in the end her and her prince
Lived happily ever after.
I don't want a fairy tale
Or a life that's predicted.
I don't want to play by the rules
Or have a world that's restricted.
I want to do what I want
Say what I want
And have nobody tell me otherwise.
I don't have to pretend
Or stick it out to the end
'Cause I'm tired of all the lies.
Some girls have a dream
That can't possibly be
Some girls want Prince Charming
But that is not for me.
I'd rather rock a rave
Than a cotillion ball
'Cause the dresses and jewels
They mean nothing at all.
I don't want a fairy-tale life.

**Kelly Marshall (13)**

# Alice

Now silly Rabbit tricks are for kids
and I hope if you're a kid you won't ever understand this
There's too much attitude hanging around
too much hate, too much pain
too many negative sounds
I don't . . . live in a hood, or a ghetto, or a block
but you don't have to be Alice to know which turtle is mock
I know . . . that I can't stand
to even look through the glass
at this world that I'm seeing
I want my Wonderland back
This whole thing started with Dum
and it'll finish with Dee
but my world keeps on shrinking
I can't stop it from crushing me
The Hatter's proud . . .
He's like a cat with the milk
The Queen plays ignorant . . .
lives in her palace of guilt
This is my voice
why won't you listen to me?
It's not a game, not a toy
this isn't my fantasy
So I surrender . . . to this land that's so wonderful
I thank God . . . for this land so free
You gotta stop . . . get down on your knees
No tricks now, Rabbit . . . it's time to listen to me.

**Leanne Rutledge (17)**

# Untitled

We've been sat here for ages,
Reading textbook pages,
I have dreams of wages, you know . . .
Want to listen to the teacher? No!
Just think of making money . . .
It's one of my dreams, honey,
To swim in a sea of green,
Even though I'm just a teen.
It's my dream, honey,
To make me a lot of money.
Tests are pests,
Ban revision,
Rather watch television.
Give me a job,
I'm no slob.
I'll be your maid
As long as I'll get paid.
Just think of making money.
It's one of my dreams, honey,
To swim in a sea of green,
Even though I'm just a teen.
It's my dream, honey,
To make me a lot of money.
Designer fashion,
It's my passion!
Blowing all your money,
Wouldn't that be funny?

**Frances Coakley (14)**

# Already Gone

My parents are screaming but I can't hear a sound,
Nobody else knows cos they're never around,
I try not to listen, I just close my eyes,
Sit and remember our happier times.
And so I'm packing my bags, getting ready to leave
Because I'm the child that they never believed.
Leave behind the pictures, I still have the memories.
Looking on the Internet at different cities.
Escaping this life for once and for good,
I would never do it if I didn't think I could.
My friends don't believe me,
I'll show them wrong,
It won't be long now till they find I've gone.
And so I'm packing my bags, getting ready to leave,
Because I'm the child that they never believed.
Leave behind the pictures, I still have the memories.
Looking on the Internet at different cities.
My bags on my back, I'm nearly out the door,
This is more than I've ever wanted before.
People are looking, but I couldn't care less,
If they want to find me, they'll have to guess.
And so I'm packing my bags, getting ready to leave,
Because I'm the child that they never believed.
Leave behind the pictures, I still have the memories.
Looking on the Internet at different cities.
I encountered a lady, she asked where I'm going,
I simply replied, 'I'm already gone.'

**Hannah Stoddart (14)**

# If Music Be The Food Of Love, Chocolate Must Be a Symphony

I ain't chasing dreams no more
Cos I'm standing in one place.
The notes ain't flowing from my hopeful core,
Why is it so hard to face?
The dream is over,
It wasn't meant to be.
How wrong was that four-leaf clover
That bitterly lied to me?
Everyone makes mistakes,
That's why they put rubbers on pencils.
I'm gonna take a break, cos I've got arm ache.
I bet all you guys think I'm mental,
You put the you into improvement,
But just cos I don't care, don't moan, I don't understand,
The only thing is, my head is up in Neverland.
The beauty in this competition
Is that you can write any type of song,
Go on an emotional expedition,
And yet still never be wrong.
It would be great to see Beyoncé
Or Jaycecott,
But Amy Winehouse's fiancé
Has took off with the lot.
Inspiration,
Interpretation.

**Eve Pardoe (12)**

# Never Mine

I'm not perfect, I never will be,
But I really wanted you to see the real me.
I guess we never got a chance,
Even with all the time we had.
Never mind all the reasons,
I still  love you for who you are.

I need you to be here today,
Cos I'm just not that independent, baby.
This could be our little secret,
Ooh, oh, no pressure, but this love we can't forget.
I promise we'll never regret.

I hope you were proud of me,
Of what you wanted me to be,
Because I am proud of you,
I swear it's true.
Please just know, I wished every single night
There was something I could do,
You are and always be my favourite person,
I will always love you.

I need you to be here today,
Cos I'm just not that independent, baby.
This could be our little secret,
Ooh, oh, no pressure, but this love we can't forget.
I promise we'll never regret.

I love you but you're never mine.

**Beth Potts (14)**

# Leaving

*(Dedicated to Adam, my fantastic friend, who has moved to the other side of the world permanently. I will miss him dearly.)*

You are my beautiful mess,
You guide me through the year,
You take away my stress.

You are the person that I call,
When it's three in the morning
And I'm about to fall.

Sometimes we disagree,
But in the end, you stick with me.

You are my one and only man,
Who treats me like crap
'Cause you know that you can.

You are the single sweetest guy,
Who can still make me smile
After you make me cry.

And tides may change,
But in the meantime, you're always on my mind.
Although our bond can fade,
I'll still be sitting here, looking at the stars, thinking of you.

And so it may seem
We're more than just friends, you're such a good friend to me.
In the end, and after all,
You're my one and only, my sweet guy, my yellow shining star.

**Isabelle Chevalier (17)**

# Show Me Love

*What is love?*
*Can you tell me?*

Contentment and happiness, I already know
Loss and betrayal, confronting our foe
It's not like I'm short of emotions
But what can earn my devotion?

I long for the passion that comes with young love
To fly high and giddy on the wings of a dove
The meaning of soulmate I can't understand
To know love at the touch of a hand

I'm a stranger to love, I'm yearning to feel
The things I've experienced are nothing so real
And I've heard that the greatest thing you'll ever learn
Is just to love and be loved in return

They all try to tell me that my time will come
But I want to meet with love while I'm young
I want those long days together
Hoping it will last forever

I'm a stranger to love, I'm yearning to feel
The things I've experienced are nothing so real
And I've heard that the greatest thing you'll ever learn is just to love and be
loved in return

*So what is love?*
*Can you show me?*

**Abigail Warwick (15)**

# The Love For You

I see you next to me,
like a star, but doesn't blind me,
just look at me, but please don't go, please don't go.
Oh, oh,
If you are the one that I love
we could have lots of fun
with many parties and music.
All the night clubs and noise with the boys
then I go and meet you
and go and have lots of fun with you.
If you get lost, I'll find you
if you're sad, I'll cheer you up,
I've fallen in love,
don't leave me now,
just don't leave me.
Oh, oh.
If you are the one that I love
we could have lots of fun
with many parties and music.
All the night clubs and noise with the boys
then I go and meet you
and go and have lots of fun with you.

All the love is in the air tonight
because I'm in love
with you, with you,
oh yes, I love . . . you . . .

**Jacob Marklew (14)**

# Give To Others

Think of all those people
On lonely streets
With no clothes to wear
And no food to eat
Next time you're gonna be negative about yourself
Think about your good clothes, good food and good health

Think about yourself
Living in luxury
And all those people out there
Who don't have necessities
Which they really need to live
There's so much you could give
To help them

Think of all those
Local charities
All they need
Is a little money
Next time you're gonna be negative about yourself
Think of your good clothes, good food and good health

The next time you walk past
That charity shop window
Think again
Stop, go back
Go in
And give to others.

**Ailish Crombie (13)**

# Life Of A Broken Heart

Broken into pieces,
crushed beyond compare,
dying seems like comfort
as you're choking on the air.

It feels like part of you is missing,
like your spirit isn't there,
like your soul was killed within you,
like you're one half of a pair.

Your smiles don't stretch as far,
your eyes are dried of tears,
your laughs are not as loud,
like facing your worst fears

Your wings are ripped and shattered,
your wrists are slashed and red,
and hope for something better,
seems lost among the dead.

You're torn up and you're shaken,
you're battered and you're bruised,
everything seems dark now,
you're so lost and confused.

The pain beats through your veins,
as the torture begins to start,
the end of everything you loved,
the life of a broken heart.

**Madlen Cartwright (16)**

# Yearning

A thousand shattered pieces
Broken beyond a heart's repair
What did I do to deserve this
Except love what wasn't there?

I thought that you were different
You weren't like those other guys
But no, you turned out just the same
Oh, what a big surprise

I guess I should know better
It's not like you're the first
I swear, sometimes I feel like
Where love's concerned, I'm cursed

You tricked me with your kisses
And your loving, gentle touch
But other than your lust for me
There wasn't very much

I thought you really loved me
But I guess that I was wrong
I thought that we were special
But you were stringing me along

And now I'm lost, alone again
I don't know what to do
I know you only used me
But I was in love with you.

**Francesca Di Georgio (16)**

# Wii Song

All the Miis in the town
always walking up and down
driving along on Mariokart
hitting your opponents with a dart!

Yo! The Wii is so cool
you will be a total fool
if you do not have this tool
it would just be plain cruel!

Learn to cook with Cooking Mama
you will not be cooking llama
learn to dance with pop star Hannah
her second name is Montana!

Yo! The Wii is so cool
you will be a total fool
if you do not have this tool
it would just be plain cruel!

Now you will have heard some games
you will not forget the names
of the games in this song
or else look in Hong Kong.

Yo! The Wii is so cool
you will be a total fool
if you do not have this tool
it would just be plain cruel!

**Annie Benton (11)**

# Tell Me The Meaning

What is the meaning of life
When all that you feel is the pain that it brings?
Even when you're at an all time high
There's bound to be something to drain everything.

Where is the point in trust?
It's gained, maintained and soon it's lost
Just try and control your emotion
Keep a hold of your heart, whatever the cost.

Where is the point in respect?
It's given to most and never returned
I suppose that it should be expected
But once it's lost your lesson is learned.

What is the meaning of hurt?
Everyone's bound to experience bad times
From broken hearts to open scars
The pain that arises when family and friends die.

What is the meaning of greed?
We need to sit, reminisce on what we've lost
We're lucky enough to have what is needed
We should be thankful for all that we've got.

What is the meaning of love?
It means so much 'til it's taken away
Although it can make you so down and depressed
It still makes you smile at the end of the day.

**Aaron Hall (16)**

# This Break Up

It always happens when you least expect it,
The dreaded words, 'We need to talk.'
I know where this conversation's gonna end, so don't pretend,
In our journey, in the road we've reached a fork.

Now I knew this love wouldn't last forever,
Now I know it wasn't meant to be,
For me this break up isn't easy,
You never cared, but I didn't wanna see.

I close my eyes and embrace the sensation,
Let the tears roll down my face,
You'll never know how much you hurt me,
You just said, 'We weren't in the right place.'

Now I knew this love wouldn't last forever,
Now I know it wasn't meant to be,
For me this break up isn't easy,
You never cared, but I didn't wanna see.

The phone goes dead and you fall apart,
Why is it over? Didn't you only just start?
Don't tell me rubbish like, 'We have to part.'
Do you know you just broke my heart?

Now I knew this love wouldn't last forever
Now I know it wasn't meant to be,
You said you did, but I can't help but wonder,
Did you ever really love me?

**Lynette Parkinson (15)**

# Living My Dream

There is lots of darkness around me,
Open up my eyes and there's light,
People sitting all around me,
Clapping as they hear my voice.

The passion is here,
The spark feels so right,
I've just regained my energy
And I feel so . . . *alive.*

Suddenly the people are gone
And all I am doing is having fun,
My heart is beating like a drum
Because the music's just begun.

The passion is here,
The spark feels so right,
I've just regained my energy
And I feel so . . . *alive.*

The passion is here,
The spark feels so right,
I've just regained my energy
And I feel so . . . *alive.*

I'm back in the darkness,
I can see no light,
Now it's all over,
That was my dream . . .tonight.

**Fern Snailham (15)**

# Complete Addiction

My personal heroine,
A never-ceasing addiction,
The buzz I get from talking to you,
When you leave, the desperation.

Through the wind I hear your voice,
In the clouds I see your name.
Living life without you,
Just couldn't possibly be the same.

And like a complete addict,
With poison in my veins,
One day it's gonna all run out,
And all that'll be left is my love's remains.

Through bloodshot, tear-soaked eyes,
I see your face before me,
My heart screams out to you, calls your name,
But my pain you cannot see.

Sensitivity, for a gaping wound,
Sewn over so many times, just beginning to heal,
Ripped open carelessly, without thought, or consideration,
No one can begin to comprehend the pain I feel.

And like a complete addict,
The poison will run dry,
No longer will I hear your name,
There'll no longer be a need to cry.

**Joanie Hutchinson-Ross (14)**

# The Iron Giant

One normal day
In the village of Semite
There was a boy called Horvath
Walking by the sea

But just then the water
Started to ripple
Then from the depths below
The iron giant appeared

With big red eyes for eyes
And a body made out of iron
This robotic giant
Was the tallest thing for miles

The giant could be friendly
Horvath knew
So they became the best of friends
The most unlikely crew

But then the army came
The boy was scared
They destroyed the giant with a powerful missile
But nobody really cared

The giant had a special power
It had the ability to heal
Waiting to be fully fixed
To start the adventure again!

**Jameel Campbell (12)**

# The Real Me

Your imperfection is desirable,
Something you already know.
My pessimistic view of us
Has lately begun to show.

But as our eyes connect,
You can see that I'm smitten.
When you listen hard enough,
You can hear my heart quicken.

My ability to be heartless
And however numb I may be,
You stay true to your word, babe,
You carry on loving me.

I feel that exhilarating rush
As you take my hand,
One I used to joke about
But now can understand.

The change in me is due to you
As we've grown together.
I love you, as you love me,
An amount unable to measure.

Things won't stay right for long,
But I'm glad you stuck by me.
You gave me the chance I needed, boy,
To let you see *the real me.*

**Emma Callaghan (16)**

# Questions

Where have you gone?
Where did you come from?
Was it from high above,
Places I have never seen?

Was there a garden?
That place where you came from,
Was it mysterious, secretive?
Don't be naïve,

Tell me the truth,
I'll ask no more questions.
Give me the answers
And teach me a lesson,

A lesson on you,
A lesson on lessons,
A lesson on listening
To lots of things about you.

I now know where you come from,
I'm going to visit you,
I'm going to ask you some questions
'Bout that first day I saw you.

Now all I have to do
Is tell you this one thing,
This one thing, mysterious, secretive,
This one thing is . . . I love you.

**Tyler Harvey-Cowlishaw (13)**

# Let's Party, Party, Party Tonight

Let's party, party, party tonight . . .
I know you're feeling crazy
School's been getting you down
Let's chill out with the home girls
And feel that funky sound
There'll be me and you, baby,
And a rocking band too, aha
I wanna party with you . . .
Let's party, party, party tonight
Let's shake it, shake it, shake it
Till the day is light
The jam is really kicking
And we're feeling alright,
Let's party, party, party tonight
Come on and let your hair down
We're gonna lose control,
Just put on your dancing shoes now
And work that tummy roll
You can sing the blues another time
But right now leave your troubles behind
Let's boogie, oogie, oogie
Till the day is light.
Tomorrow we can worry,
Tomorrow we can fight,
Let's party, party, party tonight,
Let's party, party, party tonight.

**Amber Riley (11)**

# Never Meant To Be

My hands turned sweaty,
My mind went crazy for you.
You made me feel wanted,
You made me trust in you.
Now I see love isn't meant for me,
You made me see reality.
It made me see I can't always be happy,
All good things have to end.
You told me I was special,
You told me I was amazing,
That's a lie.
Walked in, hand in hand,
Arms round each other's waists and
All I did was cry.
I thought you'd be different,
I thought you were something new.
Really you are all the same.
I fell so hard it hurt, and I
Changed my life so you and I
Could be together.
What a waste of time.
What a waste of time.
Now I see love isn't meant for me,
You made me see reality.
It made me see I can't always be happy,
All good things have to end.

**Liana Jillians (14)**

# Ode To Indie Rock

I don't like hip hop, don't do rap,
I'd rather grunge was off the map!
Pop is not my cup of tea,
And screamo's far too loud for me!
What keeps me going round the clock?
A good old dose of indie rock!
A guitar and drum kit any day
Some catchy lyrics and I'm away
To a world of hats and skinny jeans,
Dancing away to The Libertines,
While Pixies lull me into sleep
In a place where I don't follow sheep.
Lyrics are deep, misunderstood,
Better than 'wazzup in da hood'!
The singers' accents aren't fake,
Diluted by designer makes,
It's loud and frank, the message clear,
Let it steal your soul, my dear!
Guitar, drums, bass, voice - all the parts
The beat of the song matches beat of heart.
And it's all washed down with an awesome riff!
Already I can feel the shift
To somewhere else as I sing along.
It's avant-garde, and I belong.
Some may laugh and some may mock,
But my heart lies with indie rock.

**Rebecca Grant (15)**

# Eraser Buddies

We'll have great adventures,
You know that I'll be there,
Like running through the past times
And flying through the air.
The painted faces, scary places,
They won't keep us apart,
You're always there right by my side
And forever in my heart.
Eraser buddies - yeah, that's just what we are,
We'll stand tall, when all around us
The world is falling down,
Cos we'll paint stars across the sky
And colour all around.
With the age of the flower power
And the show of the meteorite shower -
Dreams that seemed impossible but now are reality,
With fruity-tasting plastics and spacemen on the moon,
Dreams that seemed untouchable, but all became true -
Yeah, all because of you.
Eraser buddies - yeah, that's just what we are
We're filling all the corners with joy and happiness,
Bringing smiles to all the people -
You know that's what we're for.
We'll be staying together, of that you can be sure,
Cos you're my eraser buddie
And that's just who you are.

**Emma Silk (12)**

# Let Go

I remember the day I first fell in love with you,
The glisten in your eye where I realised what love can do.
The beauty, inside and out, which sparkles away,
Your smile which lightened the dark, bleak, winter days,
Your personality shone so brightly through,
The small things which reminded me of you,
The infinite times you made me smile,
The time it took you quite a while to see,
You and me.

Cos missing you's like missing me,
A part of me's lost, no one else can see.
An angel who watches from up above,
The power, the darkness which they call love,
The sunrise and the morning haze,
The sunset as light starts to fade,
The memories left of me and you,
The things that worked out just how we wanted to.

A thousand words can't describe what you mean to me,
To live my life without you just cannot be,
The tears which run right down my face
Every time each thing falls out of place,
Maybe my love was wrong and we don't belong
Together, but it fits like a simple song.
That's why I'm finding it hard to let go,
I wish there was an easier way, but no.

**Kate Stanforth (15)**

# Not Fully Grown

Pearls of tears fall down her ebony face
Eyes of amber burning brightly
Her walk starts to quicken its pace
Trying to escape

Her puffy crimson eye
His forceful fist flying 'accidentally'
Moisture escapes her eye
Why stay?

Her baby boy tottering along
Trying to catch up
He's got to think she's strong
She drags him away

Until he stops
Grabs her hand
Tries to explain
He understands

He says
'I'm not so stupid
That I don't know what you're going through
Not too young
To feel pain just like you do
And I'm gonna try to save you on my own
But I'll mistakes along the way
'Cause I'm not fully grown.'

**Zoë-Maria Wright (17)**

# A Tattoo For You

I'm gonna get a tattoo with your name on
To remind me of all our days gone
So when I see it, it takes me away from . . .
The things in my life that have stayed wrong

I'll roll my sleeves up to show the world
The shirt all wrinkled and the cuffs all curled
Red and black ink, lovehearts and swirls
A permanent stamp, my emotions swirl

I got a tattoo . . . for you
(I'll never regret it)
A tattoo . . . for you
(So I never forget it)

I grit the pain between my teeth
As the ink is hammered underneath
This tattoo will always remain
It's worth the small amount of pain

I got a tattoo . . . for you
(Always with love)
A tattoo . . . for you
(So rise above)
I got a tattoo . . . for you
(It's true)
A tattoo .. . for you
(For you).

**Luke Blunt (16)**

# Open Up

I walk along a sandy shore,
A bottle had washed up at my feet before,
I read the note that lies inside,
And realise I'm the only one
In which this person could confide;

*I hide every feeling*
*And tie it up with string,*
*For a note in a bottle, as I cry,*
*My tears make the ocean it will swim high.*
*Thoughts and feelings are music from the heart,*
*Meant to be shared and not set apart,*
*Whether you're lost and lonely, or scared and sad,*
*Don't keep bottled up the feelings you have.*

Those words, I thought, would make a lovely song,
Honest and earnest from someone so young,
But they must have felt great pain and sorrow,
Thinking of an uncertain tomorrow.

*Thoughts and feelings are music from the heart,*
Love, hate, sadness, anger, despair or fear,
*Are meant to be shared and not set apart,*
With someone dear or willing to hear.

So I say open up and let it out.
Open up and let a little light in,
Let the world know you're gonna keep fighting.

**Judith Kerr (15)**

# Walk Away

All of us the same
In many different ways,
I got your back
And I will to the end.
No matter what they say,
Never walk away,
Friends are here to stay,
So never walk, never walk,
We'll never walk away.

True ones are hard to find,
That's why I've limited mine.
You are my good friend
And always will be until the end.
As long as I'm breathing,
You can believe it,
'Cause I know what you're needin'
whenever you need it.
Best friends stick together,
No matter what the weather.
I press on night and day,
Praying you'll never fade away.
Known my girls from a kid,
Had good days, we really did.
We sat together on the street,
Waiting for new people to meet.

**Jessica O'Neill (13)**

# One Wish

If I could have one wish
I would wish to hear your voice every day
The smile that brightens up my day
The laugh to get rid of my problems
The feel of your heart beating with mine
Knowing I could never find that someone like you in my life.

**Kimberley Grewal (17)**

# An Amazing Friend

You're an amazing friend
Every day till the end
You're my guide and sunlight
Even when I'm in fright
You show me the end of the rainbow ahead
Even when I feel dead
We've fallen out only twice
Over stupid things, when you were only being nice
You're the only one I trust
Even when I leave you with the pie crust
When the skies are black and grey
Our friendship's here every day
We do everything together
People think that I'm your sister
At the moment
We're only twelve
Still building our friendship on a shelf
Best friends, that's what they say
Getting stronger every day
I love you, like a friend
Best friends till the end
You're like a flower
But you may act a bit sour
But you're my rose, to be exact
Our friendship, a gate, never to be unlatched.

**Lydia Knight (12)**

# Untitled

I need to wake up, it's a beautiful morning,
The darkness has gone and the day is just dawning,
But I
Need you there by my side.
I sat by the phone just to wait for you ringing,
I'd wait there all day and that's why I'm singing
To you.
You broke my heart into two,
So help me, I'm falling in too deep,
Wake me from this never-ending sleep.
I don't need this anymore,
I need to move on from you.
I waited for days for you to call,
Staring at your pic on the wall.
It's not fair
Cos you never cared.
Now I just lie in my bed all day long,
Playing guitar and writing this song
For you,
Cos boy, I'm feeling so blue.
So help me, I'm falling in too deep,
Wake me from this never-ending sleep,
I don't need this anymore,
Cos I need to move on from you.
Cos yes, I need to move on from you.

**Brogan Evans (13)**

# A True Love Affair

The one time I was happy
The one time I cared
He was taken away
By a true love affair
Taken away and my world came crashing down
His long brown hair
The sparkling blue eyes
The perfect smile
Stays in my head
Because of him
The music he made
When he talked to me
The night ended with true love's first kiss
True love's first kiss ended all too soon
The true love ended with a bang
That sunny afternoon in the park
The last day of summer
The car span out of control
Hitting straight into him
And he lay on the floor, not moving
His long brown hair
The sparkling blue eyes
The perfect smile
Stays in my head
Because of him.

**Louise Hughes (14)**

# Beautiful

There are so many people in the world
Who would give you anything.
Someone is around the corner
Who wants to say you are beautiful.
No matter what, nobody can bring you down in a day.
Listen to the voices in your head,
Watch what people say,
You are beautiful in every way,
I can't bring you down,
So I won't bring you down today.
Do you know someone is holding on looking for you?
Out of the door you go, making sure there's someone with you
So people just think that you are horrid,
But do you know that you are beautiful?
No matter what you say, people can't bring you down,
So they won't bring you down today.
Jump up, hold on tightly, we say,
You are the one and only beautiful thing
On my mind today.
You may not believe in yourself
But people do today.
Don't hold yourself down,
Put your head up high,
Listen to your thoughts
Because you are *beautiful.*

**Yasmin Bedford**

# You Need Aquafresh!

I woke up in the mornin'
And I smelled your breath

I say, 'Oh ah oh ah
You need Aquafresh.'

It's in your body,
It's comin' for you,
So get ready,
It's gonna kill you.

I say, 'Oh ah oh ah
You need Aquafresh.'

My teacher smoked,
She nearly choked,
It was really bad,
It made me sad.

I say, 'Oh ah oh ah
You need Aquafresh.'

My mama told
Me not to take the cig,
Because I will turn
Out to be a pig.

I say, 'Oh ah oh ah
You need Aquafresh, fresh, fresh, fresh.'

**Alan Sharif (13)**

# Not So Beautiful

The first day that I saw you,
You looked me in the eyes,
And from that moment forward
You didn't see past my disguise.
You saw it all the sweet way,
You thought of love at first sight,
But when you got to know me,
I wasn't quite as nice.

So . . . you caught me at my best,
I just hope you can accept
That I can have my bad days,
And I'm not always . . . beautiful,
You were seeing an illusion,
But now it's all confusion,
Yes I can have my bad days
And I'm not always . . .beautiful.

Just like a fisherman,
You hooked me in unknowing,
You never, ever thought
Of what I wasn't showing,
But you've gutted me and skinned me,
So there's no throwin' me back,
I don't look as sweet on the inside,
The beauty line's gone slack.

**Kate Davis (13)**

# What's Happening Today?

Boyz, boyz, what's happening today?
You used to just enjoy a friendly football game,
It didn't matter 'bout being black, white or Asian,
As long as you could play, you were included.
But funny today, now they're getting older,
They seem to wanna do things to show they're much bolder.
The divide of culture and races starts to occur
Then the forming of gangs start to prepare,
War begins and tragedies everywhere.
You get families wondering why their sons were killed.

They start going around thinking they're bad,
Because all they really need is someone to love,
Because they're so young it's so much harder to find,
So joining a gang is their way forward for a better life.
They don't understand what they're getting themselves into,
Until the top dog tells them to shoot someone close to them.
When they back down it's all on them, because
They're risking their life so they're not killed instead.
Now the time has come to make the decision,
Is it you or your cousin whose life is about to end?
The choice is so hard, the decision is yours,
You need to find help before the police knock at your door.
So make sure your decision is wise and make sure it's all the truth,
Because if you kill your cousin, your family will turn on you.

**Bushra Peart (15)**

# Blue T-Shirt

I'm wide awake and I'm dreaming of you,
I'm lying down whilst thinking of you,
I'm crying out and wishing for you,
In your loose blue T-shirt, you make me smile,
In your brand new trainers that aren't even tied,
You hold my hand and you hold me close,
I look in your eyes and I smile some more.

**Katie Addison (14)**

**178**

# Let Go

The last time that I saw your face,
I clung on tight to you.
Said I'd never, ever let you go,
but there was nothing I could do.
You told me to loosen up my grip,
and move on to someone new.
But my head just couldn't contemplate,
on ever losing you.

And I'd hold on hoping forever,
that we'd stay here together.
But I have to let go.
And I'm sorry,
that it wasn't easy.
That I wasn't stronger,
you might have lasted much longer.
I just couldn't let go.
But now your eyes are closed for good,
you've found your peace at last.
I can hardly bear to touch your things,
as it brings back all our past.
All our good times and the bad times,
as I head towards the door,
it kills me inside knowing
that there will never be any more.

**Alicia Gleeson (18)**

# Sparkling Star

You've got the style
And the smile
That makes the boys go wild!

You've got the face
And the grace
To show 'em that you're ace!

You got it all, all - all, all, whoah
You got it all, all - all, all, yeah!

So put your keys in the car
And rock that guitar

Then swing your hips,
Get to grips,
That I'm the new star!

So light a fag,
Read a mag,
Is that your whole life?

Didn't think so . . .whoah!

So get a life
And a tan,
And your super, sparkling man!

Cos you got it all, all - all, all!

**Hannah Shade (12)**

# Love Is Around

Shall I compare ye to a summer's day,
Always in a lovely way,
My heart is just for you,
I don't know what to do.

Love is in the air,
It is very rare,
Maybe it isn't true,
But I will always love you.

Love is around,
It is bound to be,
When I love ye.

I don't want you to go,
You make me laugh
Or say I'm daft,
But I will always love you.

I love you for who you are,
Not what you do,
You're here to see
I love ye.

Because I love ye
And I don't want you to leave me,
So please don't, I plea.

**Matthew Lonsdale (12)**

# Your Blue Eyes

I look up at the sky at night
It's a dark, dark blue
And then I think of you, aaah, yeah, you

The blue is your eyes
The star is that twinkle
And I know it is you

I may not remember much
But you are hard to forget
'Cause you were special
You were loving
You were you

The blue is your eyes
The star is that twinkle
And I know (I know)
It's you

When I see the sky at night
I shed a tear for what you were like
And suddenly the past comes flooding back to me
Ooooh

The blue is your eyes
The star is that twinkle
And I know it is you.

**Sinead Marlow (13)**

# Me And You, My Dear

At the beach at sunset
walking hand in hand
me and you just talkin'
sittin' in the soft, warm sand

I close my eyes, you kiss me
your fingers running through my hair
we gaze out to the ocean
breathing in the salty air

You tell me that you love me
that I'm so beautiful and rare
like Romeo and Juliet
we were made to be a pair

You wrap yourself around me
my head restin' on your arm
I know that you'll protect me
With you I'll see no harm

My fingers start to tremble
as you whisper in my ear
we'll be together forever
I can feel it when you're near

Me and you forever
me and you my dear.

**Amy Halliday (15)**

# Nine Eleven

As the two tall towers melted to the ground
In America there wasn't a sound.
An eerie silence filled New York
Everyone too stunned to talk.
People covered in debris,
The dust was so thick no one could see
The two towers that once stood high,
Now no longer met the eye.
Fire fighters did all they could,
Most of them covered in blood.
As the black cloud disappeared,
Everyone's face was drenched with tears.
People staring into space,
Imagining their loved one's face.
All of those who were lucky to escape,
Now stood behind the cordon tape.
People were starting to pray,
Hoping their loved ones would be okay.
I, for one, was not there,
But can imagine everyone's despair.
I personally think everyone
There was a hero,
As I stand here and now
At a place called Ground Zero.

**Stephanie Bean (13)**

# Let's Do More To End Poverty!

Just across the world,
Starvation kills people, you see,
Yet it's nothing to do with anorexic teens,
In fact, it's named Poverty.
Daily life is such a struggle,
With lack of food and lack of heat.
Children work from the age of six
As their parents struggle to make ends meet.
They do not have yearly holidays,
Nor nice cars or free speech.
Reality is, even essentials like water
Are unfortunately out of reach.
Some have rarely seen school,
Have never played fun games.
Considering how little they actually have,
It's surprising they have names.
They lack self-pity, continue to smile
Despite their constant sorrow.
They're the most grateful people alive
For they live for today and welcome tomorrow.
And after 15 years I finally realise
That their horrible lifestyle bothers me.
So who's with me when I say,
Let's do more to help end poverty?

**Seòna Fitzpatrick (15)**

# Turn Back The Time

Sitting here listening and waiting
Watching the world go by
There's so many things I want to do
If I could turn back the time
I'd hold on forever
And I'd try not to cry
When I saw the things that made me hurt so bad
When I was supposed to be having
The time of my life
'Cause if I could turn back the time
I'd really have the time of my life
Sitting here all by myself
I know I'd make the most of it
So, no more hiding in broken shadows
No more waiting on a shattered dream
And no one could tell me what to do
Sitting here listening and waiting
Watching the world go by
If I could turn back the time
I'd say sorry so much more
And I'd smile my life away
There's so many things I'd want to do
If I cold turn back the time,
Turn back the time.

**Alis Hales (12)**

# Redemption Rap

Hey, why don't you come sit down,
Whilst I tell you all what's on my mind?
If you look outside you will find
So many people dying . . . but why?
It don't matter if they're black or white
That's no reason to start a fight
We shoot them down
We hear their cries
There is no difference between skin and eyes
But what if you were to bump your head
And fall asleep on a tanning bed?
Would you want people to pick on you
Cos now you're darker a shade or two?
So if you were to walk in their shoes
But you wouldn't know what to do
But say
'Look, I am only of the darker nation
So I don't need this discrimination
It's not my fault, no one's to blame
Every one of us is just the same'
So don't judge a book by its cover
I know we were taught better by our mothers
To know the difference between good and bad
Not the difference between white and black!

**Kayleigh Desnos (17)**

# Long Time, No See

Long time, no see
Pure in the cell, physical in the Polaroid
Long-ripped eyes stare at past mirrors
How can they be so content?
Lines etch along purer times
Suffer from the unspoken crimes
Long time . . . no see.
I hold my regrets and loves for no one to see
And I call your name well past social acceptance
And your memory tears at me
And the guilt of innocence grates at me
Glowing, never fading
Fading robbed of the basic
Basic mocking my need
Long time . . . no see
I hold my joy and hates for no one to see
The only comfort I seek impossible to give
And so I say; long time . . .
Long, long, long time no see
Time to see gone by
Gone
Long time, no see
Why won't you come back for me?
Long time . . . no see.

**Helen Russell (16)**

# Check Me Out More

Ye, ye, ye,
You check me out,
Two kids, a husband,
Was a venture scout.
Living in this flat . . .
What a drag.
Man downstairs
Smoking his fags.
Women next door
With a little pup,
Barkin' all night . . .
What a runt.
Livin' in my neighbourhood
It ain't that bad,
There's just knives and guns
And people in gangs.
Scared all night,
Scared all day,
Just hopin' and prayin'
That we get away.
This is the end,
There is no more.
Check me out,
You check me out more.

**Katie Baigent (15)**

# Better days

Since young I've had the mind of the old
I've been KOM since I was 9 years old
It was given out of love
Written to me from a lineless code
But I come from a block where the nights get cold
And almost every day you'd see the lights would blow
That's probably why
I'm stereotyped
As anti-social
But some nights, I cried when I went to sleep
Please don't lose respect
'Cause crying don't mean that your soul is weak
It's an expression of compressed rage
And this is the only time you're gonna see my emotions
Written on such a blessed page
But when I slept, my mother would confide in me
Saying, 'Son, you aren't gonna lose respect
'Cause in this world you don't owe any man a debt
In John 11:35 it said even Christ, 'Jesus wept'
That gave me hope
If Christ can do it, then I don't feel shame
Anyway, if he done it then I'd rather do the same
My prayer to God is to keep my mind, body and soul on
                                        a humble plane.

**Kofi Marfo Apau (17)**

# America's Lies

You're just a powerful nation based on simple microchips,
Propaganda brings brainwashing, that's exactly what it is.
Patriotism helps to recruit soldiers at the age of sixteen,
And what does the government tell them? We're living the American dream.
You silence the freedom of speech with new anti-terror laws,
You also hid the secrets of 9/11, just to provoke another war.
So here we go, I'm about to state to you the facts,
Afghanistan is the 36th country you've attacked on this map,
And what was the result? One million Iraqis dead.
Most of these women and children, they don't even own a bed.
Every day it's like the last supper for them, they're always breaking bread,
Cos another family member was caught up in the crossfire and bloodshed.
These people are mostly farmers who fled like sheep,
Who would have thought the powers of such a nation would
                                        retaliate on the weak?
See, these are the kind of secrets that your governments don't ever speak.
Bush said America's got weapons of mass destruction to seek,
And what did they find? Absolutely nothing.
The secrecy of your government, they had blatantly been bluffing.
You came to complete your mission, and that was the fall of Saddam.
A few years later we all ask ourselves, so why haven't you all moved on?
This was your mistake, cos what you're doing is wrong,
Look at the statistics, so many citizens converted to Islam,
Another bomb will probably be set off before I even finish this song.

**Jammo (19)**

# The Royal Mire

There are two tales to tell you,
One was told to me, and although
It's the better of the two
I'll focus on the other.
'Character is very apt
A word to describe such a place.
Outside it doesn't disappoint,
But in is a downright disgrace.
One part should hold the attention of all
But discomfort holds focus at nought.
Determinedly eight would speak and debate,
But few of the fine words were caught.'
It was here that I recalled
What it was I wanted to tell you
And doubtless, you'll agree,
That Rosencrantz and Guildenstern
Are, in fact, alive
As where I was sitting
Wouldn't have done the pair justice;
'Although, all was not entire bad.
An advert brought ironic cheers
From those beginning to tire.
If this is a 'jewel of Liverpool'
Then I'd hate to see the mire.'

**Michael Tapp (17)**

# On2U

I'll keep my friends close but my enemies closer and
you'll never pull the wool over my eyes again
'cause I've been played; I won't make that mistake this time.
You fooled me once and I sat back and let it be
but fool me twice, and it's just a shame on me.

You tell your stories, got them hook, line and sinker
and the crowds believe every word you say,
it's all just lies,
every word that falls from your lips.
I won't be bought, not ever, not tomorrow, not today.
They all linger on your words like it's poetry
and everyone feels for you like your tears are real
but every word is just another try for attention,
it makes me wonder just how insecure you must feel.

I'll keep my friends close but my enemies closer and
you'll never pull the wool over my eyes again
'cause I've been played; I won't make that mistake this time.
You fooled me once and I sat back and let it be
but fool me twice, and it's just a shame on me.
You go around frontin' like everything you say is true
but it's too late now, we're all onto you.
What goal did you ever hope to achieve?
We all know that your stories are make-believe.

**Dannielle Brickley (18)**

# Finding Me

I wonder at times, if I'd ever lose my mind.
I'd make everyone see that this is not me.
I'm willing to break, and be my own self,
So is there a trace? Cos I need to find this place . . .
Where I can hide away . . . through a world beyond lies.
The countless times are the pointless rhymes
That I just seem to hold on to.
And it's clinging to me, like the salt in the sea.
What's become of me, is not me . . .

So I'll take all my chances
And push them along,
Try to find a reason as to where I belong,
Cos I'm not sure where this is leading.
Just holding on . . .
To things I believe will make me damn strong.

And if at times I lose this feeling inside,
I'd be sure to carry a smile on my face,
Cos I'm willing to break, and be on my own.
Can anyone find me this place called home?
And the countless times that I've tried . . .
And the pointless rhymes I can't let go of
Are clinging to me, like this leaf on a tree.
What's become of me, is not me . . .

**Hasina Begum (17)**

# End Of Time

I thought it was the beginning
Suddenly it turned colder
When I see you standing there with her

You came and
Went again and
Left me standing there
Thought that it was
Only
Just the start

Thought you were gone
How comes you came back to me?
I keep going round in circles

You came and
Went again and
Left me standing there
Thought that it was
Only
Just the start

Now it's time for you to go
And for me to move on
My mistakes will make me
Strong.

**Amy Walker-Roy (15)**

# It Was All A Lie

Nobody saw the way my heart needed you,
I was so alone, perfectly invisible.
And when you smiled at me you made me feel
Beautiful, amazing, absolutely invincible.

Cos I didn't know that it was all a lie,
You didn't even really realise that I was alive.
You led me on, then you pushed me down,
And I was so in love, I didn't see that
I was begging for you from the ground.

So when you asked me out,
A part of my heart knew it couldn't be true.
But the other part was only beating for you so I said, 'Yeah.'
I was so in love with you.

Cos I didn't know that it was all a lie,
You didn't even really realise that I was alive.
You led me on, then you pushed me down,
And I was so in love, I didn't see that
I was begging for you from the ground.

So when I saw you with her,
You shattered my world.
Would it have hurt so much
If it were any other girl?

**Katarina Blow (13)**

# Just Close Your Eyes

Freckles of light shine upon this time.
When all you see is the dust,
As your dreams fall away,
You know it's gonna be okay, somehow,
But in the morning you can't believe your dreams are gone.
You know you won't be fine, just crushed.

Just close your eyes,
It's not real, baby.
Wipe your eyes to get rid of those runaway tears.
Hold on tight and don't let go.

People believe that there is so much more to reality,
Than just waking up and doing your daily things.
But people make mistakes.
Imagine the things we would see if we knew how to take control,
How we would believe to follow our dreams.

Just close your eyes,
It's not real, baby.
Wipe your eyes and get rid of those runaway tears.
Hold on tight and don't let go.

Just close your eyes,
You don't have to believe anymore,
Just hold on and let your dreams take you places.

**Lauren Dobson (16)**

# It's A Big World (But There's No One To Talk To)

You're a solid rock on the outside
Who everyone looks up to
But as wise words are spoken by you
Your problems are on your mind

Rejection and loss are your biggest fears
All you can feel is your saddened pain
Feeling life is just a hard old game
But you're losing and the end is near

All you want is someone who will listen
A friend who you can trust
But they never understand and throw you in the dust
Someone you think is helpful, but isn't

It's a big world but you feel so alone
No one you can talk to
Never anyone who will love you
And you don't want to be on your own

But although you feel life is tough
Don't change your life for anyone
Just be true to yourself and have fun
Be yourself and love every day.

**Michelle Harris (14)**

# Trapped Inside Your Love

Something as simple as a word,
or as subtle as a smile,
just to let me know you care.
You know, it's funny, I've heard
all the excuses and lies
a million times over before.

I have to break free,
I need to let go
cos it feels like I can't breathe.
I'm trapped, yeah, I'm trapped in your love,
just maybe I'm stuck, I got hooked
in your arms.
I need release
to be freed from your hold,
cos baby, I'm trapped,
yeah, you got me good.

You know that feeling you get
when someone's let you down?
It's exactly the same
whenever you're around.
All the hurt and the pain
when I've realised you've gone and done it again.

**Bianka Hannam (15)**

# Everything, Always

I'd climb mountains to be by your side
Bear the worst of weather, just to look in your eyes
I'd swim the largest oceans, the stormiest seas
A smile from you makes me weak at the knees

I'd be your friend when you could no longer stand
I'd be there when you were sad
I'd be everything you wanted the most
I'd be your everything, always.

**Johanna Lewis (16)**

# Dark Justice

I see no, hear no evil.
Readless writing on the walls
I see a million faces,
And one by one they fall.

Is it black-hearted, evil,
With no brave-hearted hero?
Just pass me your hand,
And I'll show you who *I am!*

Go ahead and try to see through me,
Do it if you dare
You take just one look at me
And I freeze you with one stare!

I see and feel the evil,
My hands will crush them all
You think you can beat me,
I'll laugh while watching you fall!

Will you remember me?
Do I capture you or set you free?
The decision is not up to me
That's who I am
It's just dark justice!

**Reece Martin (13)**


# Guess What?

It's time for me to spread my wings and fly,
Nothing to hold me back now,
Without you, my limit is the sky!
All you did was act stupid and make mess,
Your annoying laugh, your bad jokes,
Your friends and them boozy blokes.
To me you're just extra stress!
So if that's what you thought . . . good guess!

**Katie Clarke (13)**

# As Strong As You

There's a voice inside of my head
And it's always telling me what's right and what's wrong
There's a voice inside of my head
And it just won't let me out
No, it just won't let me out

I'm trying to find my own path
But how can I be my own person?
When you are always telling me what to do
Always telling me how to act

I've gotta be the person that I wanna be
I've gotta see the world through my own eyes
I've gotta do what I wanna do
Because I'm just as strong as you
Yeah, I'm just as strong as you

So why don't you just stop trying to be the controlling one?
Why don't you just leave me alone?

Because I've gotta be the person that I wanna be
I've gotta see the world through my own eyes
I've gotta do what I wanna do
Because I'm just as strong as you
As strong as you.

**Laura Saxon (15)**

# When Two Hearts Become One

Now I only have half a heart
Because you stole the other part
When you spoke to me
When you looked at me
If only you felt the same way
Maybe you will someday
Because my heart is yours
Because I am yours.

**Richard Mitchell (17)**

# Lost

Ladies and gentlemen, I've been trying to think of a new song
But I can't get my head around it, it's like I'm a bit lost . . .

All these bands around the world make it look not so bad
But it's making me look so sad.

A lot of bands, they can do great work with their imagination
But all you're getting from me is just hes-hes-hesitaiton.

I'm lost, I can't really, really remember
I haven't got much time, not even till September.

Solo singers, they know what they're doing
So I've got to get ready and I've got to get going.

Come on brain, do what you gotta do
I can't give up, I've got to get this through.

I've gotta keep in the game
I've gotta show no shame.

Lost, lost, there isn't much time
There isn't much ink
Just give me a moment, I need some time to think.

Wait, wait, wait, wait . . .
I got it . . .

**Matthew Dempsey (10)**

# The Streets I Live

People walk past us with smiles on their face
But deep down they're thinking, *you're a disgrace.*
The streets are a place where hard kids meet,
But really they're surrounded by the heat
But when you've got the gun in your hand
The gin rush kicks in and your life is banned
I know this boy whose girlfriend, is only 13
She's got her own baby but she don't seem keen.
Learn by your mistakes.

**Atlanta Wood (13)**

# Love Potion

It's my love potion, it only belongs to you,
When you drink my potion
It'll make all you see true.
You'll feel everything I feel and
Everything I know,
And if this final thing don't work,
I will have to go.

There're times you feel you can't go on
'Cause everything you feel is wrong,
You just have to dig down deep
And hope that love will find its feet.

We all have those moments in time
When you just wanna say, 'Be mine,'
But that love they just don't get
And dwell on that time that they first met.

So you do something that ain't right,
But it means there's no fight
And the darkness turns to light,
As long as you remember . . .
It's all to win the heart
Of the one you love.

**Michael Quigg (16)**


# Dreams

I love having dreams,
No matter how real it seems.
Me and a prince in castles,
Wearing dresses with lots of tassels.
Robots coming over hills,
Suddenly turning into tills.
Planets like Mars,
Looking like stars.
I just love having dreams.

**Camille Young (13)**

# Figure It Out

I always seem to be in the wrong time zone,
At this rate I will never find home.
I take the blame for everything you've done,
When will you see what you have become?
Take your time, walk, don't run,
Until we remember how this began.
It takes more than a walk, talk and pout,
When will you start to figure it out?
I wish we could just start it again,
I take the blame for everything you've done.
When will you see what you have become?
Take your time, walk, don't run,
Until we remember how this began.
It takes more than a walk, talk and pout,
When will you start to figure it out?
When will you start to figure it out?
I take the blame for everything you've done,
When will you see what you have begun?
Take your time, walk, don't run,
Until we remember how this began,
Until we remember how this began,
Until we remember how this began.

**Adrienne Lee (13)**


# Our Life

What would you do if your first love had gone?
Who would you hug if your life went wrong?
What would you do if there was nothing left to see?
How would you live if it weren't for me?
Would you make a path within your head
To help you think when your brain goes dead?
Would you run away if you had a home,
Or would you prove to everyone
You can make it on your own?

**Lauren Richardson (12)**

# Searching For The Meaning

Happiness, pains and memories,
What do they all mean?
Should we believe everyone we meet?
Everyone we see?

Love, laughter, why?
Everything dies in the end.
Where do we all go?
Life is a mystery.

Darkness of my life
Or is it my mind?
Is there a brighter place
In this cruel world?

What is the meaning of life?
If we have to fight for courage,
Fight for freedom,
Fight for love?

What? Where? When? Who? Why?
Are the questions I ask,
But the answers I can't find.
I'm searching for the meaning of life.

**Hannah Kane (14)**


# A White Christmas!

Snow falling all around,
Soft and pretty, not a sound
Children playing, having fun
Throwing snowballs, as they run.
The fire roaring, hot with heat,
As the families warm their feet.
So go outside and play,
Here comes Santa's sleigh!

**Jessica Walsh (12)**

# Hole Made By A Mole

You are the only one who can fill the hole,
I am the mole who made the hole,
That hole in my heart,
I struck it with a dart.

I made a mistake,
I ruined a chance I can no longer take,
I shut you out,
Now I am in an emotional drought.

I'm putting my hands up, I did wrong,
You have been gone way too long.
I need you,
I am sorry for our row,

I will not do it again,
I know the times I have done it is more than ten.
I know I was selfish,
This has all been very hellish.

Oh please take me back,
Sorrow is something I do not lack.
I am the mole who made the hole,
You are the only one who can fill that hole.

**Lois Robb (13)**

# Murder

I can't feel anything,
No pain, no guilt, nothing.
I know what I did,
Just wish I ran away and hid.

But now it's all over,
I'd better run for cover.
The blood won't stain,
Won't splash over the cane.

Because it wasn't me,
So why do I still have to flee?
Dizzy with the thought,
I can never get caught.

But there you are, just led,
I think you might be dead.
I'm still stood over you,
Should I be gone too?

They found the blood,
Didn't think they would.
So now it's done,
Both of us are gone.

**Abbie Mckenna (13)**

# Song

Things just aren't working out right now
Everything changing somehow
Love never goes right
Not even in my dreams at night

There's an amazing boy
He brings me love and joy
I think he's my world
But things are yet to be unfurled

When I am with him my heart skips a beat
When he is romantic I find it very sweet
I want to spend forever with him
Without him my life would be dim

One day we will be together
No more problems, not now or ever
We will cuddle every day
Making it last until our final birthday

Things could just get better
Even if it's rainy weather
At the moment life seems like one big chore
But if I'm lucky, things will be the same as before.

**Alice Moss (14)**

# Loving Boy

There's a pretty angel,
She lives up in the sky.
A boy told her to look out for me,
And she said, 'Yes, but why?'

He said 'Cos she's my baby,
My morning, noon and night.
I love her with all of my heart
And want to hold her tight.'

The angel told me all of this
While we drank tea.
I want to go and meet this boy
And thank him for loving me.

So I went and met this kind, sweet boy,
He was such a nice guy,
Then he got down on one knee
And all I said was, 'Why?'

He said, 'Cos you're my baby,
My morning, noon and night.
I love you with all of my heart
And want to hold you tight.'

**Tamsin Ross (14)**

# Words

They remain a constant, a part of you
Acknowledging a love, expressing a hurt,
Without their sound, I search blindly
Without them we are lost, speak to me.

They were your last resort in confession,
Your first defence in innocence,
Sometimes spoken freely - a naked reality
But they were always there, speak to me.

Silence so resounding is crueller than deceit
Even the words you gave to others
Penetrated a distance, revealed an actuality
Trust, sacrifice, speak to me.

You expect me to understand a change
A change I have not seen, cannot hear
One that has made us dumb, empty
Alone I fail, speak to me.

I will not mind, if you so choose
To honey a truth, embellish a reason
Tell it as you wished it to be
I ask you only, speak to me.

**Megan Brownrigg (17)**

# Utopian World

The recession is a beast and there's nothing we can do
We just sit around our houses consuming Tamiflu

Fighting in pointless wars we know we cannot win
While MPs' expenses make the public purse so thin

Climate change accelerates but people don't believe
About the global catastrophes which we all receive

Shops are closing down everywhere you go
Yet bankers' bonuses escalate and continue still to grow

Binge drinking, drug taking, happens everywhere
Suppliers count their money and do not really care

Stabbings and shootings happen every day
The lives of naïve teenagers is the price we have to pay

Racism still surrounds us, which we can hear and see
By wacky, crazy citizens just like the BNP

A Libyan mass murderer released after eight years
Leaves victims' families speechless, reliving all their fears

So look into society, and prepare yourself in case
You find some unwanted answers about our Utopian human race.

**Cory Dunnigan (16)**


# Once, Twice . . .

You hurt her once, you hurt her twice
Then want her back for more.
She thinks you're great, she thinks you're cool
But you just treat her like a fool.
You tell her lies, you call her names
And play your underhanded games.
You've broken her heart, her spirit too,
Yet all the time she still loves you.
Please walk away and let her be,
And give my sister back to me.

**Samantha Wright (14)**

# Our Song

Time passes by but I get through,
I knew I'd be alone and without you.
The words they just come out, it feels so wrong,
My hurt's an inspiration to our song.

And oh,
It shouldn't be like this.
And oh,
I'm longing for your kiss.
And oh, I am fading like the sun,
Parting from the stars to find the one.

It's hard going on day by day
And I am not religious but I pray,
I look up to the sky, the clouds above,
And in mind I ask the angels, show me love.

And oh, it shouldn't be like this,
And oh, I'm longing for your kiss.
And oh, I am fading like the sun,
Parting from the stars to find the one.
And oh, I am fading like the sun,
Parting from the stars to find the one.

**Maria Howson (18)**

# My Fairy Tale

Prince charming, I want you to know,
I love you even though
I am no princess or a queen,
I'm an ordinary girl, not a dream.
I want to live a happy ending,
I know it won't happen
So why start pretending?
I am too plain, too boring, too strange,
I can't be your princess,
And I know that won't change.

**Poppy Barr (11)**

# Times Don't Change

With the world in the state it's in,
Not many people get the chance to win
The hearts of the ones they wait all night for,
The ones they spend their life looking for.
And all right, I guess the world's uneven,
But that doesn't mean that we can't free them
From the starving hunger and the poverty,
But the world is just too blind to see.

Our lives are full of happiness,
We're the lucky ones but we couldn't care less.

Times don't change, this is still the same,
Every desperate little girl doing anything for fame.
But that doesn't mean that they are feeble,
Really they are just normal people.
When we try, we do our best,
Don't tell me we do anything less.
In the end I know we aren't the same
And to me I think it's such a shame.

Because we are filled with happiness,
We're the lucky ones but we couldn't care less.

**Taylor Wright (15)**


# Heartbroken Girl

Her heart's all broken and clawed away
but from deep inside
she'll have the guts to say,
'Don't worry, I am fine, just a little grey,'
But she's a heartbroken girl
all torn and frayed.
And there she'll lay day by day
because the rain will fall
at least one more day
before she picks herself up and walks away . . .

**Gemma Wells (12)**

**213**

# This Thing Called Love . . .

I don't love you,
It's someone else,
And I know how it feels
To not be loved back.
I admire the fact
You love me and not her
But this guy is just my type.
He hasn't made a move,
I guess that we have in common.
I should confess my feelings
You did, I suppose
So I can be straight with him.
I guess what goes will go,
Now I know he doesn't love me,
It just wasn't to be.
So now that I'm in your shoes,
I'll cry myself to sleep.
Maybe I really do love you,
I need to get things straight.
It's painful and confusing,
It is this thing called love.

**Emily Dodds (13)**

# A World Apart

What can I do?
I ran out of room
I played my cards all wrong
What can I say?
It all went away
My head's run out of words
Maybe we're the same
No, we're not the same
Me and you are something
Me and you are worlds apart.

**Alex Heptinstall (15)**

# Lost In Your World

I used to lay dreaming of the days we once had
They had passed and I was sad
But you were gone, I had to move on
I felt like my life was one big con
Long-lost memories, nowhere to be found
But slowly and surely, without a sound
The creature of darkness was coming for thee
Now there's no one here to rescue me
So here I am, against my will
Lost in your world, grieving still
But then I realised, I've been living a lie
With my head in the clouds, on a high
You weren't the one, I was wrong
That is why I've written this song
So now I know
Not to feel so low
My piece of the jigsaw finally fits
I now live by my wits
Your world is now mine too
Cos here I am, it's in my will
Found in my world, finally fulfilled.

**Charlotte Gosling (14)**

# The Endless Journey Of Life

As the day brings in the night,
Another day has passed me by
And it all seems like a journey that won't end.
But as I sit and look above,
I see there's something that I need
And I know I can't reach it alone.
So as I'm searching for the someone
I realised the truth,
You've been standing there beside me all the
time.
'Cause you've been my weakness, you're my
strength,
You're the one that keeps me going through it
all.
Through the bad times, through the good,
You were always there for me
And you can help me reach that something that I
need.
So now the journey's not so long,
I've got you for company
And I know that I can reach it now you're here.

**Caitlin Thompson (13)**

# Stuck In Reverse

Waiting for the call that could change her life,
Worrying about her life in the fast lane,
Watching the world spin so quickly by,
So she occupies herself by playing a game.
She's just a small girl in a big world,
Can't help herself being stuck in reverse.
Stuck in reverse, ooh,
Stuck in reverse.
Thousands of people screaming her name,
Tours worldwide and showered in fame,
Feeling the rhythm and belting out songs,
Learning the words still she can't go wrong.
She's just a small girl in a big world,
Can't help herself being stuck in reverse,
Stuck in reverse ooh,
Stuck in reverse.
Can't wait for the concert to end,
Wishing she was back home with her friends.
Feeling lost in a lonely world,
Can't help herself being in reverse.
Stuck in reverse.

**Rachel Jackson (13)**

# I Still Remember

I still remember
The final touch,
The final kiss,
The very last time I felt your lips.
Why did it have to end like this?
Couldn't we have just stayed in that everlasting bliss?
Every day all I think about is how it used to be,
All those days and nights that felt like eternity,
How short it all was in reality,
Just a single bright day in the dark night,
And now I have to face the world alone,
Without you to rely on
And hold my hand.
I pray it was quick and you didn't suffer,
That death took you quickly into its arms,
I hope you're still here watching over me,
And are proud of what you see,
Because I still remember
The final touch,
The final kiss,
The very last time I felt your lips.

**Chloé Forsyth (15)**

# Lyrics

I'm standing on a hill
Looking out on the view
This is not what I wanted
Where are you?
You think I really meant it
When I told you how I feel
The drink had taken over
You know it wasn't real

So come on, let it go
Gimme one more chance so I can show
It is really love and without I feel low
Together forever you know, you know, you know

Looking out into the world
I feel so alone
I think, want and need you
But you turned off your phone
I know I was an idiot
But I can make it right
I'll love and care for you
Through days and nights.

**Bethany Smith (12)**

# To Daddy

Daddy, we'll miss you for evermore,
We'll never forget your engine's roar,
Cars and bikes, you loved them both,
But we know you loved your family the most.
Daddy, we think you are the best,
So much better than the rest.

You sang to us as we drove in your car,
Your smile brought happiness into our hearts,
We used to watch films, cuddled up close,
These are the times we'll miss the most.
Daddy, we think you are the best,
So much better than all the rest.

You made us laugh with your funny jokes,
We were so proud when you gave up the smokes.
You took us to loads of really cool places,
Which put big smiles on our little faces.
Daddy, we think you are the best,
So much better than the rest.
Daddy, we'd love to kiss you once more,
Daddy, we'll miss you for evermore.

**Sophia Ingley (12) & Rhys Ingley (9)**

# Untitled

I'm hesitating
My heart is racing
Can't seem to keep my mind off of you
Thinking about it
I'm so astounded
Just can't keep my mind off of you

Because I know it's crazy
And I know it can't be real
Don't believe in love at first sight
But you're always on my mind

They tell me I'm stupid - 'Girl don't be foolish,'
But you're mine and I'm gonna put up a fight

You're the one I wanna be with
Only one I can dream of
Got me head over heels
Boy, I'm falling in love with you
It's the way that you smile
That twinkle in your eye
Boy, I am falling in love with you.

**Keisha Christie-Morgan (14)**


# Shining Light

Baby I've seen the rain
I feel your pain
I know you need me there
I ain't going nowhere
You keep yourself locked inside
Baby, just let your heart decide
I'll be with you whichever path you choose
You're always gonna be my shining light
Through the days and lonely nights
I'll always be there to hold you tight
My shining light.

**Natalie Verrill (14)**

# You And Your Falling Blossom

Do you know what's in my heart?
When the blossom is falling
It calls our name,
Like the wind
It can erase my pain.
The blossom is calling me
Tonight . . .
You were my guiding light
But now you're just part of the night.
Before blood is spilt
I need you to know
You're always in my head,
Your eyes cutting through my veins,
Your deadly smile . . .
You don't care about these words,
So don't cry, babe,
I'm already dead,
As blossom-tainted blood
Is dissolved in the pain,
Demolished by your never-ending pain . . .

**Em Humphreys (15)**


# Don't Cha

*(Inspired by Pussycat Dolls 'Don't Cha')*

Don't you wish your boyfriend was French like me,
Don't you wish your boyfriend had an accent like me,
Don't cha
Don't cha baby
Don't cha

Don't you wish your girlfriend had a croissant like me
Don't you wish your girlfriend had a beret like me
Don't cha
Don't cha baby
Don't cha.

**Ben Catt (14)**

**222**

# I'm So Lonely

I'm so lonely, I need to be with you.
You were my friend, but you
had to go, and you left me alone,
and I'm so lonely.
All the times, they were the best,
but now you're gone
away, from the west.
I'm so lonely, I'm so lonely,
will I ever be your friend,
or do you have someone in plan?
Now you're gone away from me,
it is so hard to believe.
Now you're gone and I'm so lonely,
please, oh please, please
come back to stay, it will be OK.
Whatever you do I'll be very pleased,
but just remember
to come back to stay.
I hope our friendship is still the same
as on from today.

**Tiffany-Jayne Bull (13)**


# Untitled

I'm looking for that lightning flash
I'm waiting for that thunderclap
Thinking about the dangers inside
Knowing in my heart I'll never die
Now I'm checking for the whistle blare
Sitting on the hard ground, I'm unaware
Of the last words spoken in my name
Before we enter the final game
Now I'm scared at the idea of defeat,
Or not . . .

Looking.

**Matthew Johnson (13)**

YoungWriters

# I Hate The Way

I hate the way you ignore me
It makes me want to cry
I hate it when you choose them instead
It makes me want to die
I hate your lack of memory
And that you don't believe in fate
I hate it when you hurt me
You're supposed to be my mate
I hate the way you ignore my feelings
And pretend that they're not true
I hate that you're so perfect
At everything you do
I hate when you correct me
And make me feel less smart
I hate it when you get angry
You know it breaks my heart
I hate it when you laugh at me
And make me feel so small
But most of all I hate the way
That I don't hate you at all.

**Hannah Price (14)**

# Love

Love is a boy who has his mind on a girl,
He can't speak,
His lips are a zip.
He trips and stumbles, but doesn't twig
That she never notices him.
He can't think,
He only has her on his mind.
She laughs and looks at him weirdly.
He falls and dreams,
Then wakes up.
He's heartbroken. (9)

**Ellie May (9)**

**224**

# Making This World Mine

In the looking glass, do you see what I see?
A girl who is trapped and wants to be free.
A tree grows up to the sky and spreads out its branches,
I want puzzles and journeys, intrigue and romances,
So I'll spread my wings and I'll soar,
This little bird will fly right out that door.
I know it takes courage, and I know it takes time,
But I'll conquer this world and I'll make it mine.
I run into the wind and don't follow the pack,
I'll chase adventure and danger, won't wanna come back.
Who wouldn't want to travel the world?
What kind of place is this for a girl?
Can't wait to jump and take that first step,
Unlock the box where my dreams are all kept.
I know it takes courage and I know it takes time,
But I'll conquer this world and I'll make it mine.
Patience is a virtue
But freedom is my dream,
To change this world for better
And change my world for me.

**Megan Evans (17)**

# Rock Star

When I was a little girl
I always wanted to be a rock star,
A rock star, yeah, yeah,
So I'm, so I'm gonna become a

Rock star, I'm gonna be number one.
Yeah, yeah, a rock star,
I'm gonna be in the charts, yeah, yeah, yeah,
Oh, oh, oh, oh, oh, a rock star baby, yeah,
A rock star.

Finally I'm a rock star,
I'm really famous, yeah.
I'm gonna be a singer, no guitar,
I'm gonna be a famous superstar.

Rock star, I'm gonna be number one,
Yeah, yeah, a rock star,
I'm gonna be in the charts, yeah, yeah, yeah,
Oh, oh, oh, oh, oh, a rock star baby, yeah,
A rock star.

**Olivia Bannaghan (8)**


# Run Away

Look honey, I gotta tell you something,
I want you to just shut up and listen.
I love you and you love me too,
So why don't we just run away
From this hell of a place?
Let's go and find somewhere that is ace!
Then we can find a little cottage house there,
Oh, oh yeah, this we should have done earlier.
So what do you think?
Will you come or not?
You will? That's great,
So pack your bags cos we're . . . running away!

**Isabelle Rayworth (10)**

# Different Ways

You don't see everything going on in your mind.
You don't see anything I try to make you find.
There's a lot more things in life that you do not realise
And you do not know these are essential things in life.

We all see different ways.
We are all part of mankind, and all these different days.
The stars and moon are always burning bright.
We all see different ways in life.
We all see different ways, different ways in life.

I try to tell you different ways things can be solved.
You don't see anything I try to make you find.
There's a lot more things in life that you do not realise
And you do not know these are essential things in life.

We all see different ways.
We are all part of mankind, and all these different days.
The stars and moon are always burning bright.
We all see different ways in life.
We all see different ways, different ways in life.

**Aaron Peart (13)**

# Trapped In My Mind

Sitting in my room,
Thinking 'bout you,
You would be my perfect groom.
When you looked my way
On that bright summer's day,
What was I supposed to say?
I was in a bind,
You were trapped in my mind,
To this very day.
What do I do now?
Where do I go next?
I'll figure it out somehow.

**Emma Calvey (14)**

# My Dark Something

Heart of ice but eyes of fire
Hold me in the darkest night.
Something new
I just knew your hips moved right.

Keep your heart,
Keep your head,
Something new to dread.
Something I just can't define,
I want to make you mine.

Take a bite but you can't taste,
Think of me when you hold them.
Someone new
I knew your heart would condemn.

Keep your heart . . . (vampire)
Keep your head . . . (werewolf)
Something new to dread.
Something has to drop a sign,
I want to make you mine.

**Zoe Mackey (16)**


# Love Was Made For Us

You made a star of me
That night we were together,
Felt special for once,
When you showed me
How much you really love me.
Now there's just one thing to say,
Love was made for us,
I can feel it every way.
Now you've made me believe it,
Love was made for us.
Yeah, love was made for us,
Yeah, love was made for us.

**Kennedy Stanley (12)**


**228**

# The Fight

I've got sweat building up on my brow
And my heart is beating
And I'm thinking of cheating
I'm looking at this mess and thinking, *how*?
I'm remembering what I've been told
But my heart is aching
And my soul is breaking
And I'm starting to feel cold
I can hear the crowd screaming
But I keep thinking I'm dreaming
I'm in the middle of the ring
And I hear the *ting*
I'm looking down at my feet
And I can smell the defeat
I can hear the voices in my ear
And I know that my rival is near
I look down at my hand, I'm holding a knife
And look up at what I'm up against
And what I'm up against is life.

**Jade Jeffreys (13)**


# The Smile

Every time that we meet in the street
Your eye catches mine,
And we smile.
Your smile could light up the darkest place,
Your smile,
Oh, your smile!

People will mutter and judge us,
But we shouldn't care what they say.
Go with the flow
And follow your heart,
Follow it all the way.
Follow it all the way.

**Bethany Dolphin (14)**

**229**

# Tired Of The Rules And Everything

That I can't do,
Everyone has an excuse to tell,
But why not spit it out and say,
'You're too young to do this,
You're way too old to do that.
Pick up the slack,
Stay in line, do what you're told.'
I don't want to be told what to be,
I want to be me,
Join the revolution
Just to break free,
Step out of line for one time,
Be yourself, that's all you can do,
Excuses and lies and saying wrong lines,
Oh why won't you accept
Everyone messes up,
But because we are teenagers,
We don't get a chance,
Just want to be me!

**Hannah Boal (12)**


# Exceed Your Limits

If you don't feel there's any need
To become strong and succeed,
Your colours will fade away,
You will feel blue the next day.
Take a big stride,
Fill yourself with pride,
Exceed your limits
And everything fits.

Take some time,
Cross that line.
Take some time,
Cross that line.

**Georgina Barrett (17)**

**230**

# Snow And Death

Death is like snow
While the winter glows
Beautiful but oh so cold
Silent
Soon to be still forever
Seems complicated
But it's really anything but
Brings endings
And allows for beginnings
Has enchanted many
With its pure beauty
Has destroyed many
With its perilous cold
It can hurt
And it can heal
It's always different
Unique in every way
Never done before
And will never be done again.

**Niamh Darling (14)**

# A Sentimental Note

A winter's midnight ne'er I see,
A face as deadly quite as she,
It seemed like love blossomed true,
As my heart bloomed with words so sweet.
My voice she stole with her tender eyes
And at that place, I was complete.

Her dark eyes pierced my soul,
And she filled a part of me whole.
I knew she would forever be mine,
As my heart bloomed with words so sweet.
Her silky hair fell upon her back
And at that place, I was complete.

**Alex Merrick (16)**

# Trapped By Fame

All the girls are up in here
and all the boys are over there
everybody said, 'Hey, hey, hey!'
everyone looking at me
I mean life ain't been too easy
but my mama always said,
'Don't let them in your head.'
But I can't help it
all the cameras and media
they started getting greedier.
I'm trapped by fame
lost in time
trapped by fame, aged 29
I wanna get out
but they follow me around
somebody call 999
I'm trying to escape
but everyone knows my name
I'm the girl trapped by fame.

**Ella Jenkinson (13)**

# Puzzle Pieces

Just put the puzzle pieces back together
You'll find the reason for that in the end,
'Cause everything has a meaning and an answer,
it's not great confusion or a trend.
'Cause practice makes perfect,
It's not an assignment . . .
Or a project,
Sooo,
Once you've found the piece you're looking for,
Oh, oh, oh,
Just put the puzzle pieces back together,
Back together.

**Hannah White (12)**

# Summer Nights

The summer nights, they seemed so great
The chats we had, the fun we made, it all seems so far away
We've all moved on to yesterday
Never forget the love you had for the friends we made
'Cause we both know we'll see them some day
All the late nights, all the silly fights, the songs
The jokes, the best friends . . .
It's such a waste, it had to end
The memories will never die, they'll always be inside our minds
Oh that summer, that summer night
Best days of our lives . . .
Jumping on the last train, in the pouring rain
It was all worth it in the end
When the sun went down and the nights were dark
Sitting laughing in the park - now summer's gone
One thing's for sure
We'll make more, more summer nights
Lots more to come in sight
But that great beginning will never end.

**Sara Henry (13)**


# Untitled

Holding you tightly,
We realise the end is near,
But knowing we'll be together,
I have no fear.
Like flowers at bloom,
I know that eventually we'll wilt,
So let us carry on enjoying us,
Free from any pain and guilt.
Listening to the flutter of your heart,
I just want to hold you even more.
The taste of your mouth, the warmth of your hand,
More than I have ever loved before.

**Claire Hunter (18)**

# Dreams

The moments when my head deceives the world
As a picture-perfect thing,
The way the waves will crash upon the shore,
It's more than we dared to wish for.

It comes alive at night to find me gone
Inside, away to hide,
My dreams, these things that move my mind,
I'm stuck in my place, apart from the rest of the race.

Tell me I can't, I'll beat the game,
Toward the fame, I'll walk to the gate
To open the dream that he believes is out of reach,
Ignore the speech,
Dr Suess once riddled me a theme,
A dreamy flashback with us three,
It's okay, that's ace, just follow me.
If there's one thing I know,
It's that we need to follow our dreams . . .
Is that we need to follow our dreams.

**Tom Di Domenico (17)**


# The World Hasn't Spoken

Sometimes it's hard, sometimes it's rough
You sacrifice your life but it's never enough
The tears that we cry, the pain that we feel
It feels like a game but it's not, this is real
I look around us and I think this is a happy place
Nah, I really can't see it, all I see is a disgrace
Kids on the streets and hearts that are broken
I see the words but has the world really spoken?
It's time to make a choice of what life gives
Because this is the way I want to live
Sharing the pain with people I don't know
It's the way that I roll, so come on, let's go.

**Lauren Townsend (15)**

# I Miss You

When we're apart day after day
I just lay here feeling pain
Nowhere to turn and no one to go to
I just lay here all alone
But now night is here
I can make believe you're here

You walk with me till dawn
Together we are forever
And I know it's only in my mind
That I'm talking to myself and not to her
Still I say there's a way for us
But then all of a sudden you disappear

And now I'm all alone again
Still and waiting in this silence
Day after day I just lay here
I miss you
Nowhere to go and no one to go to
Waiting for you to be here.

**Ellie Cameron (14)**

# Untitled

Hands touch
Hearts race
Cue the fireworks right on time
Pulses race
Lips touch
I think I'm falling in love
See the stars shining bright
I'm gonna remember this night for the rest of my life
Ohhhhhh, I think I'm falling for him
Ohhh I think I'm falling in love.

**Luisa Scialpi-Sullivan (14)**

# Gorgeous Princess

She is like a butterfly,
She is top of the sky.
She always looks down on me.
No matter how fast I run,
She will always catch me.

She is a gorgeous princess,
You always have adored her.
She's too perfect for words to explain.
I-feel-so-insane
I-feel-so-insane
I-feel-so-insane
How can you blame me for feeling this way?
You once loved me like the way you love her.

In her castle she will rise
And become top of the sky.
She makes me feel so afraid.
I have already lost you once this way,
Some part of you is still safe in my heart . . .

**Tara Lewis (15)**

# Letting Go

I am holding on,
Won't let go, crying in the dark
And I feel she is watching me . . .

People always stare
As the tears roll down my cheeks
But I know she is watching me . . .

The pain I've been through,
All of the memories, I just can't let go
She still, she still, she still is
Watching me, yeah . . .

I know I have to go,
Get on with my life, but I can't, I just cry
And I feel she is watching me . . .

The loss I have had,
All the good times we had, I just can't let go
She still, she still, she still is
Watching me, yeah . . .

**Abigail Cookman (12)**

# Clear To Me

Now it's clear to me, it's happening,
It's gonna be like this forever
And it's clear to me it's never
Gonna be back like that again,
And it's clear to me
That we can be
Happy in our separate ways,
But unfortunately,
It won't be
To . . . gether.

It wasn't meant to be,
It's now clear to me,
As you can see
I'm breaking free,
So let me go, we can't be happy,
But unfortunately
It won't be,
To . . . gether.

**Sophie Mitchell (13)**

# My Best Friend

Look,
It's been two years now and I can't let go,
I wish you were here, Fred, I need you to know
That I love you still and I think of you
Every single day, and I miss you too.
I need you here right by my side,
Babe, me and you were ride or die,
But you died, it wasn't your fault, it was that man,
Couldn't get his way, so he thought he had a good plan,
Murdered you, your sister and your mum,
Did what he did, two years to this month.
Sleep in peace my angels, July 2007,
12th, that's when Fred, Bev and Kesha went to Heaven.

**Stevie Wade (17)**

# Love Is All I Lived For

Every time I wake up in the morning,
I look out of my window and gaze at the meadow,
It tells me something good about life each day,
But every dream I think about starts to fade away.

Love is all I lived for,
Love is all I need,
Love is all I lived for, cos I want you to know.

It was not long ago when we first me,
You looked straight into my eyes, I'll never forget
About the things we did together,
About the things that made me stay,
About the things we learnt together,
Every night I sit by myself and say

Love is all I lived for,
Love is all I need,
Love is all I lived for, cos I want you to know,
Cos I want you to know.

**Oscar Wenn (12)**

# Sinners

I looked across to see a
Group of sinners,
They were bad people disobeying the rules;
Doing graffiti and making fires
And they laughed at me for being who I am.
In school they laughed at me, once again.
I prayed in the toilets, amen.
I asked them, 'Why are you being so mean?'
And they laughed at me for being who I am.
I was good, not bunking off.
They were bad, taking off.
Someday I wish they'd be like me,
But they laughed at me for being who I am.

**Orlaith Comer (13)**

# Friends Are There

Friends are there for you
Friends are there for you
Friends are there for you

Any time
Just give them a call
They'll come running to you

Friends are there for you
Friends are there for you
Friends are there for you

Friends stick up for each other
They'll never tell a lie
Friends are always there

Friends are there for you
Friends are there for you
Friends are there for you

*For you!*

**Amy Barlow (11)**


# The Truth About You

I've known you for ages
I know you from school
Every time I look at you I feel like a fool.
You're cute, you're hot, you're everything I'm not,
But why can't you see you're the one for me?
We're in the same class but you've got another lass.
She's tall, I'm small,
She's blonde, I'm brown,
Every time I look at her I have to frown.
Now this is where the story comes to an end,
At the moment I'm with my bro's best friend.
He might be fat, he might be thin,
Who cares? He might mean everything.

**Megan Patton (13)**

# Untitled

I ain't no player, I work for my dough,
All I try and do is keep my rhythm on a flow,
I ain't very lazy and I'm not laid back,
All I aim to do is keep my life on track.
I've started to realise my head is set straight,
What I wanna be, it just can't wait.
I'm gonna be on a stage doing my thing
Throwing out lyrics that are fit for a king.
I've got thousands of fans too strong to contain,
All the other rappers drop their heads in shame.
I walk through the city, fans shout my name,
They get the pens and paper out, it's all the same.
They look upon me like I'm some sort of hero,
When I know I started out from nothing but a zero.
If I could give any advice of a target that could be met,
It would be to get yourself on the right mindset.
I'm going to have to love you and leave you, I thank you all,
And if you really like me, then give me a call.

**Tyler Pardo (14)**

# Because I Promised You

I've banished the puppeteer, she pulls my strings no more,
I'm gliding free from a thing called love.
I arise from an awakening first my thoughts of despair
But I'm now full of hope, knowing you won't be standing there.
You try to seduce me with shimmering eyes,
All I see is your bewitched pride,
As I pull out my shield of honour
That is full of captivated thoughts from my friends.

I realise I don't need your prayers to make amends,
But still I promise I will be there,
Through thick and thin, I'll be a breath of fresh air,
But not for you to walk on me with thorned boots,
But just because I promised, and that's the truth.

**Robyn Horton (17)**

# Never Forget You

Me and you are like a winter's day,
All wrapped up and cosy and will always stay.
Whenever I'm alone it's never the same,
But when I'm with you it feels like fame.
Every day I wake up wondering what to do,
Because I can't do anything without you.
I can't understand why you died,
Because you were so kind.
It's not fair, because no one knows how I feel,
My heart will never be able to heal.
I sometimes feel like you are around,
But you will never be found.
I never thought it would end like this,
Because I never got my last kiss.
I remember the day you caught my eye,
It never felt like a lie.
So from this day forward, I will never forget
The first day we ever met.

**Amie Sawdon (13)**

# Some People

Some people do sport
While others just sit around
More people listen
But some just make sound

Some people like sweets
Some even sour
Some are weeds
But some are flowers

Some people like dogs
As others like cats
Some like rats
But others like bats.

**Tamaryn Phipps-Jones (13)**

# You've Changed

What was wrong could never be right
Tension, obsession, becoming aggression
You've changed
I'm not holding onto this light anymore
Beginnings and endings
Are the same
It's just the start of your
New twisted game
Just one thought before you decide
On your new perfect life
What was wrong could never be right
Face it, we made it, we changed
It will just never be right
Holding on . . . losing grip . . .
Afraid this is it . . .
What was wrong could never
Be right
You've changed.

**Victoria Kyle (16)**

# Angels

Angel's protecting me from above,
Helping me to find love.
He shines a pure light above my bed
So I have sweet dreams in my head.

With clothes as white as snow,
Where he came from we don't know,
'Peace be with you,' he whispers in my ear,
So angelic and calm whenever he is near,

Hate and anger escape my body by his touch,
And when he's in Heaven again I'll miss him very much,
One thing he has taught me during his time,
That harmony can be anyone's, including mine.

**Ellie Hill (12)**

# Tim's Story

Once I was the new boy around,
Tim, that's my name,
Never long on the ground,
Always up for a game.
My best pal, Jessie, would never leave,
Or so that's what I thought.
I have known her forever,
Even from her cot.
We used to laugh and sing and play,
I hoped it would never end,
But one day they're all grown up
And you they will offend.
Replaced by gadgets, make-up and boys
And the latest trends so,
No longer does she need toys
For I used to rest against her head.
Now I'm the lonely little teddy bear
That got pushed underneath her bed.

**Hannah Craig (15)**


# Inspiration

Inspiration is what sparks your creativity,
It helps pursue your goals in activity.
My mum once said, 'Inspiration is the thing that makes you think.'
After that she picked up another vodka shot to drink.

Inspiration is the umbrella that keeps me dry,
From the raining reality which causes people to wonder and die.
Inspiration is the people on the telly showing us what is possible,
But the likelihood of normal folk is quite improbable.

The games we play from dusk till dawn,
Will one day make us tired and yawn,
But still we play till our inspiration is dead,
Until a courageous act of inspiration is back in our head.

**Callum Parker (14)**

# Broken Heart

When I look at you,
I see the moon in your eyes
But because you are gone,
I can't see it any more.
I wish you would come back,
Back to me, back to me,
I miss you so much,
Why won't you come back home?
I have always loved you
And I thought you loved me too,
I was crushed when you left
And now I have a broken heart.
Why did you have to leave,
Why did you not stay?
Now I sit at home on my own,
Thinking of you all night.
So why don't you come back,
Back to me, back to me?

**Emma Nott (12)**

# Hollow

Cross my heart and hope to die,
Hopefully someday time will fly
With a pocket full of sorrows
As my heart deepens and hollows!

My life isn't a very good book,
So if I was you I wouldn't take a look,
Half my family are far behind,
Looking for emptiness I can't find.

Bright, sunny days turn to dust,
As people have to dig for trust.
Fighting harder than ever before,
Just building yet again another locked door.

**Megan Kenyon (13)**

# Don't Be Sad

Are you feeling sad?
Well in no time you'll be glad.
Just have some fun
And don't be glum.
I know you cried,
Just put your problems to a side.
All I want to see
Is just about to be,
Just turn that frown upside down.
If you be happy
You won't be sad,
You'll be glad.
You wouldn't have cried
Even if you tried.
Evening if it's raining,
Nothing will be paining,
You'll just be happy,
So please don't be sad.

**Nimrah Haq (8)**

# Heartache

It's time for me to go,
It's obvious I'm not wanted,
Your love for me has ended,
It's time for me to leave.

It's going to be so hard,
But I'm sure I will survive,
I thought you were the one,
But I thought wrong!

It's hard going out,
Seeing our friends in love.
When I am all alone,
They're all still in love!

**Martha Robinson (13)**

**246**

# Forever

I didn't want it to turn nasty,
I hate seeing you like this
I just want to give you a hug,
I just want to give you a kiss,
I need to know that you'll be okay,
I want you to know, I'll be here forever.

So if you need a helping hand,
No matter when, no matter how,
I want you to know I'll be here forever,
No matter how far, no matter how long,
No matter what it takes . . .
I'll be here forever.

So if you need me, if you want me,
All you need to do is call me . . .
Write my number in and I'll be there,
And I will make it better . . . I promise I will,
I'll be here forever.

**Bethaney Picton (12)**

# A Typical Evening

The puffins fly slowly through the soft summer air,
As if they were quite content, without a care.
The near ocean sends waves to the cliff side,
The sun's light is showing though it had died.

The few soft clouds travel through the light,
The seagulls nestle together on a quiet night.
The small, lost rowing boat bobs on the waves,
The tiny, dart-like fish rest in the foamy caves.

Every so often, dolphins leap to the sky,
Snapping up fish as they go by.
And sometimes upon a mild, hushed evening,
You can hear the soft whistles of a killer whale dreaming.

And when one sits upon the dreary hill above the sparkly sea,
With hands kept warm and satisfied with cup of raspberry tea,
You can truly see the puffins fly slowly through the soft summer air,
As if they were quite content, without a care.

**Eleanor Hynds (14)**


# Heart In My Hand

Holding on to the secrets of my casket's fortune,
I didn't know another way.
I'll just carry on walking forever,
Wasting away.
This sacrifice is worth twice your sweet talk,
But it tears me up inside.
I'll trap myself in my own delusions,
But never mind;
I'll run until the world stops turning,
Escape to a place where there's no hope of returning . . .
My mistakes will be erased
By the sunlight of my better days;
I'll follow the stars withy my heart in my hand
And I'll be saved.

**Chloe Morris (16)**

# Memory Of You

The memory of you
Still fresh inside my mind,
The sight of your eyes,
Thank God that I'm not blind.

The smell of your skin
Still lingers in the air,
The sound of your voice,
As if you're still there.

The memory of that day
When everything was good,
You were smiling that smile,
But then you changed the mood.

The memory of you
Still haunts me to this day,
But however sad I am,
I wish that you could stay.

**Erin Cox (14)**


# Hope Is Mine

When I look in the mirror,
What do I see?
A failure,
A disappointment,
A sad excuse,
That's me.
But the birds still sing on
And the sun still shines,
So I keep faith alive.
Hope is mine.
I can be better.
The whole world could be,
If only they could see
The real me.

**Lola Oseni (13)**

# The Rainbow

You may be hurt, tired and alone, alone, all alone
You may be starving right down to the bone, to bone, down to bone
But know that just beyond the sunrise
I'll be there waiting for you.

Look at the rainbow, it shows my hope for you
Look at the stars, look how they shine for you
Look at the sun, its rays light up the world for you
Splash colour over an empty sky

You never told me why you ran away, away, ran away
Your friends and family don't know what to say, to say, what to say
They've given up searching but I still believe
That you'll be coming, you'll come to me

Look at the rainbow, it shows my hope for you
Look at the stars, look how they shine for you
Look at the sun, its rays light up the world for you
Splash colour over an empty sky.

**Jessica Strike (15)**

# I Miss You!

I miss you
You were all I had, all I ever hoped for
I believed in you and you believed in me.
I could tell you everything I hoped for
And everything I dreamed.
I miss telling you what you mean to me,
You were that somebody who gave me
That special feeling inside
And I need it back.
And now you're gone I feel the pain,
Like they stole my life too.
I just need you.
I just need you back 'cause
I miss you!

**Maria Thomas (14)**

# I Have Changed, Says The Dark Lord

Yes, I am the dark lord and killing is my game
I don't care about Harry and his so-called fame.
Yes I try killing Harry every time,
He doesn't understand he lost my prime.

Do you think he would talk if I asked him to?
Or try to kill me, like I would do?
It is true, yes, I kill for fun -
I've got a wand, not a gun.

Fun and excitement, amusement and awe,
A scar on his head is what we all saw.
I don't want it anymore, causing people strife,
I just want an ordinary, stress-free life.

I don't want people to quiver at my name,
Don't they understand I am full of shame?
So please let it end, I won't kill anymore,
Of my future I am definitely sure.

**Joanne Whatmough (14)**

# People Always

People always hurting
People always swearing
People always shouting
Shooting, killing, mugging
All the adults complaining
The news always talking
Recession, youth crime
What is the world coming to?
Making the world better
People always smiling
People always talking
People always laughing
This is what the world should be about.
So why is the world this way?

**Tasha Griffin-Hudson (14)**

# Cavern Of Love

Out there they may hate you
Or cry out your name
None of that matters to me
When you're safe in my arms.

Come out of the winds of the world
Feel the fire of my love surround you
Let your fears and cares melt away
You're safe in my cavern of love.

In this world full of changes
And inconstant life
I'll be there for you
Your anchor in the storm.

This cavern of love never changes
I will be there for you
When your world out there crumbles
There is safety within.

**Sarah Chesterman (18)**

# Jingle Bells (Updated)

Jingle bells!
The turkey smells,
Santa's already been!
Oh what fun it is to ride
On a sleigh that's never been seen!

Oh, jingle bells! Jingle bells!
Now it's Christmas Day!
Santa's been, the presents are here,
Guests are on their way!

So! Jingle bells! Jingle bells!
For the last time with some cheer!
Santa's working hard with his elves,
Making presents for next year!

**Aaishah Rauf (13)**

# These Are My Reactions

Rhythm and emotion intertwined
made into a story, a memoir, a flowing rhyme
a lyrical discovery created by the memory
a lyrical attack, on the world who can't fight back

This is life
this is the dreamt reality
this is the shadow forcing me . . .
to react.

Comfort and inspiration
the melody keeps us going on
the sound of a soulful voice . . .
makes our mind open to the destined choice

This is life
this is the dreamt reality
this is the shadow forcing me . . .
to react.

**Radhika Vara (14)**

# A Poem For Lucy

This world, a world of wonders,
Its beauties seldom told,
Like the changing of the seasons
Or the mountains growing old.

The cherubs' song at first light
And the river softly flowing,
Or a wild flower like yourself,
Untamed and ever growing.

Your petals spilling colour
Far across this land,
Yet your love so hard to catch
Is falling through my hand.

If only I could keep it,
So that we need never part,
For it's your glories and splendours
Which complete my heart.

**David Patterson (15)**

# Finding A Reason Why

It is awkward and silent; I am scared to talk
Our hands dangle aimlessly as we just walk
I do know love, and this isn't it
How do I tell you? I'll crack in a minute

I bite my lip so not to talk about what I think
We both look ahead; no exchanging looks, no knowing winks
I know you are trying hard not to mess this up
But I can sense not too long before our time is up

And kissing you brings no happiness, no joy at all
It is a relief when the end of the day comes to call
I am thinking I am with the completely wrong guy
But I don't want to hurt you, yet I don't want to lie

I can't help but worry, cos I know it isn't right
I am starting to look at life in a new light
I am so frikkin' confused about what I should do
I know I am not, and never will be, in love with you!

**Helena Bonici (15)**

# What's Close To Me?

What's close to me?
You are,
Can't you see?
Close to me.

What's happiness to me?
You are,
Can't you see?
Happiness to me.

What's love to me?
You are,
Can't you see?
Love to me.

What's the world to me?
Nothing.
Can't you see?
You are everything to me.

**Joanna Mason (14)**

# You Make Me Smile!

My little sister ought to know
That every day I watch her grow,
Even though I go away,
I'd think of her throughout the day.

That cheeky smile and long brown hair,
She'd run around without a care,
But all at once her running would stop,
As she falls to the floor in a giant strop.

Never mind, it never lasted long,
As she stuck out her little pink tongue,
And pulled a funny face at me.
I laughed with happiness and I filled with glee.

But what I love most is seeing her face,
As up the garden path I pace.
She knows who it is, she knows who I am,
I'm her big sister, who takes her out in her pram!

**Ashleigh Houston (16)**

# Frozen In Tears

She hears something at the window frame,
She doesn't let it in, in case it's pain.
Alone she sits in her empty house
Locked in from what there is out.

Dark and cold is her house so black,
Why, what does she hold so tightly back?
She holds her heart, her heart so cold
Broken by hurts and pain so old.

The window shatters with a cry
And shafts of light come from the sky,
And carried on a shaft of light
There is a bird, a bird of white.

'Tis a dove, gentle and calm,
It flies to her outstretched arm.
And there it sees her broken heart
And does become the missing part.

**Lydia Sharpe (14)**

# If You See Me, Don't Be Afraid

When you see me,
If you see me,
Don't be afraid . . .
There's nothing left for you to fear . . .

Forget about the wrong choices
That you have made,
Cos I've made mistakes too . . .

I see you when you get scared,
Don't run away . . .
Cos I'll be there to support you

So when you see me
If you see me . . .
Please . . .
Don't be afraid
There's . . . nothing left for you . . .
To fear . . .

**Cali-Leigh Stuttard (16)**

# Looking Out The Window

There are so many things
You can see looking out of a window,
Things that can't be seen
By skimming by.
When I look properly
The sky seems like a long river
With swans gracefully gliding across it.
Trees so tall, almost touching the sky
And the leaves and branches growing
Outwards on both sides,
Swaying in the strong breezes.
Cars passing by with great speed,
Old chimneys looking crippled,
About to fall like a person with no legs left to stand.
Children playing in the streets,
No cares for what lies around the corner,
Acting brave as UK army soldiers.

**Lizzy Hook (13)**

# Lotus And Pontiac

I've got an exotic and a muscle car.
I got your wheels,
You got no wheels, you got no wheels.
Wow, my exotic does lifting,
My muscle does drifting.
Swinging with my girls on a Saturday night.
My exotic lights shine so bright,
A bit like girls, yeah.
My Lamborghini girls go up and down,
Now all these women here
And the suspension in my cars goes up and down.

All my cars are pricey,
I ain't got no girls to drive the cars.
*Woo*, like like it, nah, that is all wicked.

**Jake Parsons (13), Leah Butler (12) & Ryan Price (11)**

**260**

# Finding Home

We just want a place to call our home,
We don't care what you say,
We don't care what you own,
I can stay away from family,
I can try to find a home.
So let's march to the drums,
Let us stumble past our mums,
Let us find a place called home.
As we walk through the shadows
You attack who we are,
Put us behind these glass windows
But yet we are so young,
We are smart, we are young
So we can find a place called home.
So as we find some paradise
That we can finally call home,
It's finally found, that is our own.

**Liam Hegarty (13)**

# Chance

Take a second and just calm down,
I can't see you like this
When your feet aren't firmly on the ground.
He's done it again, I can see it in your eyes,
He's been cheating and lying,
That's no surprise.
You deserve better than him,
You deserve the very best,
What do you see in him and all the rest?
You need to get out and say goodbye,
And find a man that will at least try.
One guy that will make you happy and not cry.
One person who loves you
For exactly who you are,
So just give love one more chance,
One chance tonight,
One chance will make it right.

**Jessica Whitelegg (13)**

# The Simple Life

My nose was struck by the odour
Of a shabby, homeless man,
Whose staggering steps blocked my path
And hid the rays from the sun.
It was as if the day was dying,
The clouds as the graves.
The sun slowly fading out of sight,
Leaving me in the depths of despair.
Then suddenly sunlight shone through the window,
Making stripy patterns on the floor,
Strong enough to blind you.
Pupils sat at tables eating their lunch,
Smiling and laughing, talking about
Their love life and plans for the weekend.
Out of nowhere a bell rang,
There was silence all around,
Just like my house when I go home!

**Rebecca Sedman (15)**

# Think Of You And Me!

I've seen you once, I've seen you twice
And we've known each other
For so long . . .
But how much do we really know about one another?
I don't know!
You change,
I change too,
But we remain the same . . .
At night I close my eyes and I see your face,
Your eyes and your lovely smile,
Then I'll stop and think . . .
Do you ever close your eyes and think of me?
Do you wonder if you and me
Will be together . . . ?
Next time when you close your eyes
Or sleep and dream at night,
I'll be hoping it's about me!

**Elisha Roper (15)**

# Do You Know Me?

Do you know me,
Do you see me?
Do you know me when you leave me out at night?
Do you see me? When you leave me out of sight
Do you realise that I am what you've got,
Would you leave me to stay out and rot?
I would be with you forever,
If only you would let me,
I would always
Stay right by your side
Even on
The scariest ride . . .
Do you know me?
Do you see me?
Would you know me?
Would you . . .
Ever see me?

**Tyla Thomas (11)**

# Untitled

I woke up this morning in a good mood,
Thinking I would see you,
But when I walked past you I didn't get a second look,
And all I wanted to say is, 'I love you . . .'

I went to school and walked past you
To find you with another girl,
I felt like such a fool then,
I saw you joking around with your friends
And thought, *me and you till the end,*
But I forgot to say-ay-ay, 'I love you . . .'

You walked up to me today and said
'I saw you looking at me
And wanted to say I love you . . .'
Then we were walking down the road hand in hand,
And I said, 'Me and you together, forever
And I love you too . . .'

**Ashleigh Myers (13)**

# I Will Be (Reprise)

Lay by the grass with me, darling
I want to feel your heartbeat.
Such a beautiful sound,
Shining when it's found,
The innocence it brings to me.

Listen to my soul sing, darling
It's calling you back to me,
My window is open,
So please come home,
I want you now.

I wanna be free from all of this pain, and heartache,
To hold my head up high and kiss the rain.
Lift your hands to the skies,
We'll escape these lies
And I will be . . .
A part of you.

**Katie Darragh (14)**

# Life And The Teen

So how long shall I wait for you to come around?
Cos I'm losing my grip, to stand on stable grounds.
Nothing's worse but things do take their toll, and still
                                    decide to fall.
So how do you plead, guilty on your knees?
With your hands held up high, reaching towards the sky.
No one's perfect and you're an exception,
So go and take your bow.

So how far will you go until you hit the unknown?
Ten more miles down this road, leading where God only knows.
Here's your chance, take it while you can, before it's too late.

So will you be the one to sweep me off my feet?
With your charm, arm in arm, with words that flow so sweet.
Here I am,
Take my hand,
And fly me away.

**Natasha Smith (17)**

# We Are United

You could be black
You could be white
You could be wrong
Or you could be right

If you've got brown hair
Or if you've got blonde
We all come together
To sing this song

We are united
We're all one family
We are united
As close as we can ever be
We are united
Together we stand
We are united
The power of love sits in your hand.

**Zahna Eklund (14)**

# Acoustics

The acoustics were great, the music was loud
we were rocking out to this awesome sound

When I saw you, you saw me
and we found where we were supposed to be

In your arms, by your side
you made me feel alive

I found you, you found me
in our hearts we know it's mean to be

Forever true, forever real
cos now I know the way you make me feel

When the acoustics are great and the music is loud
we can rock out to the awesome sound

In your arms, by your side
I begin to melt, inside.

**Georgina Cullen (16)**

# Song, Rhythm, Dance And No Sense Of Time

My mind is in the rhythm,
My legs are working overtime, running me into oblivion,
My heart is pumping, jumping, locking, breaking, hip-hop making,
My eyes are seeing music playing, no faces, I see only sound,
My mouth, it speaks for my heart, it talks for those that can't,
My nose is smelling things that only live in song and dance,
My ears are hearing colour, bursts of dazzle-shine,
No sense of other feelings and no sense of time.
My hands are feeling what I'm seeing, vibrations from the floor,
I live the song, the words, the poet, the rhythm that is me,
No vision-fade like black ascending staircase from the floor,
I reach the top and walk through
Distant closed doors.

**Briana Freed-Smith (13)**

# This Girl

There's a girl walking in these shoes
And she knows that everything she's got
Is all she's got to lose.
There's a dream right behind these eyes
And she finds a reason to be strong with every tear she cries
Being hard to fight the way things are
So she leaves the world behind
With the sound of doubt turned up so loud,
She turns the music up inside.

And this girl's seen a lot of pain
But this girl's gonna smile again,
She knows that a flower grows every time it rains,
And this girls' got a lot of dreams.
She knows that tomorrow ain't what it seems,
She might not solve a mystery tonight,
But this girl's gonna be alright.

**Emily Angel (17)**


# Memories Of You

Thoughts of you come frequently
Moments of you and me
It matters now how or when
Those thoughts of you are deep within me
From our special place
To our first embrace
Our first dance
To that final glance
The memories engraved
On our special stage
I think of you often
Because you mean so much
But now I bid farewell
Until our next touch
I miss you.

**Victoria Milner (13)**

# You're The One

You make me feel
As if nothing else is real,
There's just me and you in this world,
And my mind is all swirled
With thoughts of me and you,
No longer being two,
But together, being one,
While my worries all go numb.

Sitting beneath the stars
And knowing that the night is ours,
How I hate to see you cry
When we say goodbye,
And when I get those butterflies
That I didn't get with other guys,
I know that you're the one
For me, for me.

**Ashleigh Willmott (13)**


# Make-Believe

We never talk, but in my head
There's not a moment when you're not there
And we've passed more than just friends
Call me crazy, but that's just me
And I know deep inside you believe
We should be together
So why make-believe?

Just fall in love right now
Let this last forever
Just fly away
Escape it all, just you and me

There's not a moment when you're not there
We've passed more than just friends
So why . . . make-believe?

**Dimple Visram (13)**

# Winter

It always rains in winter,
Why can't there be snow?
It always keeps me awake in the night,
Rain, rain, rain.

You can't play outside
And you're stuck indoors
With nothing to do.

As soon as December starts,
You would love to see your advent calendar,
But too scared in case you wake, you wake Mum and Dad,
So wait until breakfast and rush down
And gobble up your first chocolate.

You can't play outside
And you're stuck indoors
With nothing to do.

**Victoria Jenkins (8)**

# I Know

Have you ever felt so lonely
You could cry?
Have you ever been unsure
Of how to say goodbye?
And do you mean it
When you laugh?
Are you sailing on rough water
Afloat a punctured raft?
And you ask yourself,
What does it mean?
'Cause I'm standing at a cross road
I can't see a thing.
What's the point in living
With nothing to live for?
Well, I know,
I know.

**Jack Moran (14)**

# Some Dreams

When they were children
When they were small
They had these wishes
They would share with all
They had some stories
And this is what they were
To climb the tallest
Mountain on Earth.

Some dreams don't come true
But that is right up to you
There are so many loves and wishes
Crammed up in the world
And there are so many people as well
That I can't tell
Oooh, I can't tell!

**Rosie Ellis (12)**

**274**

# Mum

Dear Mum, you're number one, this is your song.
Daddy left many years ago, but you stayed strong.
You whispered in my ear that it would get better,
You told me we'd get through all the bad weather.
You raised me and my sis as a lonely mum,
This song comes from the heart and a pair of lungs,
24/7 screaming you're number one.
You got two kids proud to call you a mum,
18 years old, I've seen what you've been through,
Making choices, brain had to think too,
Adding to your problems, sorry, didn't mean to.
Every day it's a new goal you're achieving,
You're my role model, that one I believe in.
I know I love you don't get said much,
A bond between a mum and her kids, that's love.
Show you through the music with a kiss and a hug, X.

**Jake Rogers (18)**

# Walk 'N' Talk

I've chosen the wrong course to drive
I've gotta choose my rights
My love is all due respects right now
I want you to leave
At first I thought you were an angel
Sent by the gods themselves
But that was all an act and I'm taking it all back

So you can walk your walk
And you can talk your talk
But you can walk and talk over to the door
Hey, yeah, yeah, yeah, yeah,
Grab your car keys an' take your jacket
Because they're all you're getting back
It's all you deserve for what you've done to me
Get gone . . .

**Chelsea Whitehead (14)**

# ElleBaybii

The music races through me throbbing like a heartbeat
Chillax, watch my act, take a seat.
I'm ElleBaybii, I have the ability,
Other lyricists feeling the fragility,
They ain't got the skills, they're only faking
In their size 3 Uggs, their feet are quaking
The rhyming war is a competitive rat race
Babyii's big hair vs GaGa's poker face
With her fashion senseless, she ain't got a prayer
To beat ElleBaybii you need natural flair
I ain't got a job, I'm still a schooly
Hanging with my mates and all that tomfoolery
Playing my tunes such as Taylor Swift
Swap it with Green Day, you'll cause a rift
Rascal's Bonkers sending me dizzy
Dance wiv me . . . sorry I'm too busy!

**Elle Coton (12)**


# You Don't Notice Me

You don't notice me like I notice you.
You treat me like I'm gone,
You make sure that I'm torn.
Am I just invisible to you
Or is it too obvious to see me through?
That I like you, that I like you.

Sometimes I deny it,
Sometimes I trust it,
Sometimes I think it's not true that I like you.
Am I just invisible to you,
Or is it too obvious to see me through?
That I like you, that I like you.
Am I just invisible to you,
Or is it too obvious to see me through?
That I like you, that I like you.

**Nicole Cheng (12)**

**276**

# New Life

She sits alone in her bedroom
With the music playin' loud
Her body's on the bed
But her head's up in the clouds
And she dreams that all her classmates don't laugh and jeer
And instead of broken lights, above her head's a chandelier
And she'll look into the mirror
And she wouldn't feel obscene
And she looks like the girl on the front of the magazine
Her boyfriend stars in top movies and buys her lots of gold
She's known as smart and mature and her body's really toned
But even though the dreams seem real, even she knows
That everythin' she wants won't come flying through the window
And she gets off her bed
Looks at the sun, takes in the sight
And says to herself, this is the start of her new life.

**Kayla Eber (14)**

# All You Need Is Love

I now realise that I was wrong
That the silence hurts
And it's gone on for too long

Why do you feel broken
When we are the same?
Screaming, we'll sing
'We can fix you, you're not alone.'

I now realise that I need you
Stay with me
Together we'll make it through

Why do you suffocate yourself
When we are on your side?
Screaming, we'll sing
'We can save you, you're not alone.'

**Jessica Taylorson Feitas de Melo (14)**

# Believe In Him

Without you this could never be
You gave me the chance
The chance to shine
You gave me the power to be great
You showed me the way
The way of God
To love and to cherish
The ones you love
And your neighbours, no matter what
You believed in me when others did not
You told me I could
So I believed
You helped me to achieve
In ways people couldn't believe
Lord, you gave me a wonderful blessing
And I thank you for that.

**Shanice Harrison**

# I Know A Place

I know a place where the sun always shines,
The sea always glitters,
And people's eyes always sparkle.

The place brings joy and happiness to every single soul,
It blows away sadness in a single gust of wind.

This place, however, only exists if you really believe in it,
And this is why not many people have been,
They haven't looked inside their souls, their hearts or their minds,
And so they fail to believe in the magical land I call my home.

I know a place where the sun always shines,
The sea always glitters,
And people's eyes always sparkle.

Do you?

**Tamara Davis (12)**

# The Magic Of The Moon

The moon is a wonderful, beautiful thing,
the light from it illuminates everything.
At twilight, a lone wolf stands proud,
and a lonely civilian makes no sound.
The man is not afraid of the creature he sees,
he stares into her eyes and never flees.
He knows the wolf is misunderstood
and that other people never think she is good.
He shows an appreciation for what she is,
and she begins to accept the reality of this.
He listens to her unique calling card
and knows her existence must be hard.
Her magnificent howl is enough to say,
everything she needs for him to stay.
He sits beside her in a silent embrace
and stays forever in his final place.

**Gabriella Routley (14)**

# How Life Works

Because this is how it works
And I know that it's not fair
I know sometimes it hurts
But I've learnt how to not care

I realised what it's like
And I know it's not changing
They filled us all with lies
Then decided to blame me

Now you will find out too
That it's a conspiracy
I hope it won't hurt you
But I can't make sure you see.

**Sally Coad-Jones (15)**

# That's Me

I'm the microphone killer
The lyrical thriller
I'm the master of the MC
That's what I'm like
I'm so cool
Cooler than ice cubes
Better rapper than Ice Cube
Scrapping all the old rappers
Because they're old news
I'm new, I'm fresh
I'm better than the rest
I'm in, you're out
That's what I'm about
Fresher than a summer breeze
Yeah, that's me
I'm the bee's knees.

**Reece Hudson (12)**

# About You

My friends try to choose
Who I should stay with and
Who I should lose
But this time
Nothing they can say
Can make me change
The way I feel
About you (ooh)
Every day and
Every night
You're in my mind
Can't get you out
I think it might be
Something special
I think it might be
Something special.

**Jade Wiles (12)**

# I Would

I would wait for you in the deepest hell
for you, my soul I would sell

I would wait for you in a thunderstorm,
for you I'd have my heart torn

I would wait for you in the pouring rain
for you I'd go through so much pain

I would wait for you in the freezing cold
for you I'd do anything, even when we're old

I would wait for you in Hell or Heaven
for you and our friendship I'd bring us back together

If you ever left me or go taken away,
I wouldn't bear it, you're the best friend I have

I'd face my biggest phobia just to get you back.

**Harlie Burges (15)**

# Young Writers Information

We hope you have enjoyed reading this book - and that you will continue to enjoy it in the coming years.

If you like reading and writing poetry drop us a line, or give us a call, and we'll send you a free information pack.

Alternatively if you would like to order further copies of this book or any of our other titles, then please give us a call or log onto our website at www.youngwriters.co.uk

Young Writers Information
Remus House
Coltsfoot Drive
Peterborough
PE2 9JX
(01733) 890066